Hands-On Data Analysis with NumPy and pandas

Implement Python packages from data manipulation to processing

Curtis Miller

BIRMINGHAM - MUMBAI

Hands-On Data Analysis with NumPy and pandas

Commissioning Editor: Sunith Shetty
Acquisition Editor: Tushar Gupta
Content Development Editor: Prasad Ramesh
Technical Editor: Sagar Sawant
Copy Editor: Vikrant Phadke
Project Coordinator: Nidhi Joshi
Proofreader: Safis Editing
Indexer: Rekha Nair
Graphics: Jisha Chirayil
Production Coordinator: Shraddha Falebhai

First published: June 2016

Production reference: 1280618

Published by Packt Publishing Ltd.
Livery Place
35 Livery Street
Birmingham
B3 2PB, UK.

ISBN 978-1-78953-079-7

www.packtpub.com

`mapt.io`

Mapt is an online digital library that gives you full access to over 5,000 books and videos, as well as industry leading tools to help you plan your personal development and advance your career. For more information, please visit our website.

Why subscribe?

- Spend less time learning and more time coding with practical eBooks and Videos from over 4,000 industry professionals

- Improve your learning with Skill Plans built especially for you

- Get a free eBook or video every month

- Mapt is fully searchable

- Copy and paste, print, and bookmark content

PacktPub.com

Did you know that Packt offers eBook versions of every book published, with PDF and ePub files available? You can upgrade to the eBook version at `www.PacktPub.com` and as a print book customer, you are entitled to a discount on the eBook copy. Get in touch with us at `service@packtpub.com` for more details.

At `www.PacktPub.com`, you can also read a collection of free technical articles, sign up for a range of free newsletters, and receive exclusive discounts and offers on Packt books and eBooks.

Contributors

About the author

Curtis Miller is a graduate student at the University of Utah, seeking a master's in statistics (MSTAT) and a big data certificate. He was a math tutor and has a double major in mathematics, with an emphasis on statistics as a second major.

He has studied the gender pay gap, and presented his paper on *Gender Pay Disparity in Utah*, which grabbed the attention of local media outlets.

He currently teaches basic statistics at the University of Utah. He enjoys writing and is an avid reader. He also enjoys studying politics, economics, history, psychology, and sociology.

Packt is searching for authors like you

If you're interested in becoming an author for Packt, please visit `authors.packtpub.com` and apply today. We have worked with thousands of developers and tech professionals, just like you, to help them share their insight with the global tech community. You can make a general application, apply for a specific hot topic that we are recruiting an author for, or submit your own idea.

Table of Contents

Preface

Python, a multi-paradigm programming language, has become the language of choice for data scientists for data analysis, visualization, and machine learning.

You will start off by learning how to set up the right environment for data analysis with Python. Here, you'll learn to install the right Python distribution, as well as work with the Jupyter notebook and set up a database. After that, you will dive into Python's NumPy package—Python's powerful extension with advanced mathematical functions. You will learn to create NumPy arrays, as well as employ different array methods and functions. Then, you will explore Python's pandas extension, where you will learn to subset your data, as well as dive into data mapping using pandas. You'll also learn to manage your datasets by sorting and ranking them.

By the end of this book, you will learn to index and group your data for sophisticated data analysis and manipulation.

Who this book is for

If you are a Python developer and want to take your first steps into the world of data analysis, then this is the book you have been waiting for!

What this book covers

Chapter 1, *Setting Up a Python Data Analysis Environment*, discusses installing Anaconda and managing it. Anaconda is a software package we will use in the following chapters of this book.

Chapter 2, *Diving into NumPY*, discusses NumPy data types controlled by dtype objects, which are the way NumPy stores and manages data.

Chapter 3, *Operations on NumPy Arrays*, will cover what every NumPy user should know about array slicing, arithmetic, linear algebra with arrays, and employing array methods and functions.

Chapter 4, *pandas are Fun! What is pandas?*, introduces pandas and looks at what it does. We explore pandas series, DataFrames, and creating them.

Chapter 5, *Arithmetic, Function Application, and Mapping with pandas*, revisits some topics discussed previously, regarding applying functions in arithmetic to a multivariate object and handling missing data in pandas.

Chapter 6, *Managing, Indexing, and Plotting*, looks at sorting and ranking. We'll see how to achieve this in pandas, looking at hierarchical indexing and plotting with pandas.

To get the most out of this book

Python 3.4.x or newer. On Debian and derivatives (Ubuntu): python, python-dev, or python3-dev. On Windows: The official python installer at www.python.org is enough:

- NumPy
- pandas

Download the example code files

You can download the example code files for this book from your account at www.packtpub.com. If you purchased this book elsewhere, you can visit www.packtpub.com/support and register to have the files emailed directly to you.

You can download the code files by following these steps:

1. Log in or register at www.packtpub.com.
2. Select the **SUPPORT** tab.
3. Click on **Code Downloads & Errata**.
4. Enter the name of the book in the **Search** box and follow the onscreen instructions.

Once the file is downloaded, please make sure that you unzip or extract the folder using the latest version of:

- WinRAR/7-Zip for Windows
- Zipeg/iZip/UnRarX for Mac
- 7-Zip/PeaZip for Linux

The code bundle for the book is also hosted on GitHub at https://github.com/PacktPublishing/Hands-On-Data-Analysis-with-NumPy-and-pandas. In case there's an update to the code, it will be updated on the existing GitHub repository.

We also have other code bundles from our rich catalog of books and videos available at `https://github.com/PacktPublishing/`. Check them out!

Conventions used

There are a number of text conventions used throughout this book.

`CodeInText`: Indicates code words in text, database table names, folder names, filenames, file extensions, pathnames, dummy URLs, user input, and Twitter handles. Here is an example: "Mount the downloaded `WebStorm-10*.dmg` disk image file as another disk in your system."

A block of code is set as follows:

```
html, body, #map {
  height: 100%;
  margin: 0;
  padding: 0
}
```

When we wish to draw your attention to a particular part of a code block, the relevant lines or items are set in bold:

```
[default]
exten => s,1,Dial(Zap/1|30)
exten => s,2,Voicemail(u100)
exten => s,102,Voicemail(b100)
exten => i,1,Voicemail(s0)
```

Any command-line input or output is written as follows:

```
$ mkdir css
$ cd css
```

Bold: Indicates a new term, an important word, or words that you see on screen. For example, words in menus or dialog boxes appear in the text like this. Here is an example: "Select **System info** from the **Administration** panel."

Warnings or important notes appear like this.

 Tips and tricks appear like this.

Get in touch

Feedback from our readers is always welcome.

General feedback: Email `feedback@packtpub.com` and mention the book title in the subject of your message. If you have questions about any aspect of this book, please email us at `questions@packtpub.com`.

Errata: Although we have taken every care to ensure the accuracy of our content, mistakes do happen. If you have found a mistake in this book, we would be grateful if you would report this to us. Please visit `www.packtpub.com/submit-errata`, selecting your book, clicking on the Errata Submission Form link, and entering the details.

Piracy: If you come across any illegal copies of our works in any form on the internet, we would be grateful if you would provide us with the location address or website name. Please contact us at `copyright@packtpub.com` with a link to the material.

If you are interested in becoming an author: If there is a topic that you have expertise in and you are interested in either writing or contributing to a book, please visit `authors.packtpub.com`.

Reviews

Please leave a review. Once you have read and used this book, why not leave a review on the site that you purchased it from? Potential readers can then see and use your unbiased opinion to make purchase decisions, we at Packt can understand what you think about our products, and our authors can see your feedback on their book. Thank you!

For more information about Packt, please visit `packtpub.com`.

Setting Up a Python Data Analysis Environment

1

In this chapter, we will cover the following topics:

- Installing Anaconda
- Exploring Jupyter Notebooks
- Exploring an alternative to Jupyter
- Managing the Anaconda package
- Setting up a database

In this chapter, we'll discuss installing Anaconda and managing it. Anaconda is a software package we will use in the following chapters of this book.

What is Anaconda?

In this section, we will discuss what Anaconda is and why we use it. We'll provide a link to show where to download Anaconda from the website of its sponsor, Continuum Analytics, and discuss how to install Anaconda. Anaconda is an open source distribution of the Python and R programming languages.

In this book, we'll focus on the portion of Anaconda devoted to Python. Anaconda helps us use these languages for data analysis applications, including large-scale data processing, predictive analytics, and scientific and statistical computing. Continuum Analytics provides enterprise support for Anaconda, including versions that help teams collaborate and boost the performance of their systems, along with providing a means for deploying models developed using Anaconda. Thus, Anaconda appears in enterprise settings, and aspiring analysts should be familiar with its use. Many of the packages used in this book, including Jupyter, NumPy, pandas, and many others common in data analysis, are included with Anaconda. This alone may explain its popularity.

An Anaconda installation includes most of what you need for data analysis out of the box. The Conda package manager can be used to download and installation new packages as well.

 Why use Anaconda? Anaconda packages Python specifically for data analysis. The most important packages for your project are included with an Anaconda installation. With the addition of some performance boosts provided by Anaconda and Continuum Analytics' enterprise support of the package, one should not be surprised by its popularity.

Installing Anaconda

One can download Anaconda for free from the Continuum Analytics website. The link to the main download page is `https://www.anaconda.com/download/`; otherwise, it is easy to find. Be sure to choose the installer that is appropriate for your system. Obviously, choose the installer appropriate for your operating system, but also be aware that Anaconda comes in 32-bit and 64-bit versions. The 64-bit version provides the best performance for 64-bit systems.

The Python community is in a slow transition from Python 2.7 to Python 3.6, which is not fully backward compatible. If you need to use Python 2.7, perhaps because of legacy code or a package that has not yet been updated to work with Python 3.6, choose the Python 2.7 version of Anaconda. Otherwise, we will be using Python 3.6.

This following screenshot is from the Anaconda website, from where analysts can download Anaconda:

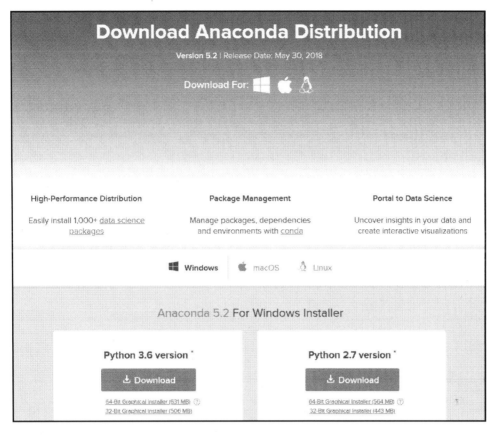

Anaconda website

As you can see, we can choose the Anaconda install appropriate for the OS (including Windows, macOS, and Linux), the processor, and the version of Python. Navigate to the correct OS and processor, and decide between Python 2.7 and Python 3.6.

Here, we will be using a Python 3.6. Installation on Windows, and macOS, ultimately amounts to using an install wizard that usually chooses the best options for your system, though it does allow some options that vary depending on your preferences.

The Linux install must be done via the command line, but it should not be too complicated for those who are familiar with Linux installation. It ultimately amounts to running a Bash script. Throughout this book, we will be using Windows.

Exploring Jupyter Notebooks

In this section, we will be exploring Jupyter Notebooks, the primary tool with which we will do data analysis with Python. We will see what Jupyter Notebooks are, and we will also talk about Markdown, which is what we use to create formatted text in Jupyter Notebooks. In a Jupyter Notebook, there are two types of blocks. There are blocks of Python code that are executable, and then there are formatted, human-readable text blocks.

Users execute the Python code blocks, and the results are inserted directly into the document. Code blocks can be rerun in any order without necessarily affecting later blocks, unless they are also run. Since a Jupyter Notebook is based on IPython, there's some additional functionality, for example, magic functions.

Jupyter Notebooks is included with Anaconda. Jupyter Notebooks allow plain text to be intermixed with code. Plain text can be formatted with a language called **Markdown**. It is done in plain text. We can also insert paragraphs. The following example is some common syntax you see in Markdown:

```
# Heading                                    Heading

## Sub-heading                               Sub-heading

### Sub-sub-heading (and so on)              Sub-sub-heading (and so on)

*italic*                                     italic

**bold**                                     bold

`monotype`                                   monotype

* List item                                  • List item
* Another list item                          • Another list item
* Yet another item                           • Yet another list item

1. Enumerated list item                      1. Enumerated list item
2. Another enumerated list item              2. Another enumerated list item
3. Yet another enumerated list item          3. Yet another enumerated list item
```

The following screenshot shows a Jupyter Notebook:

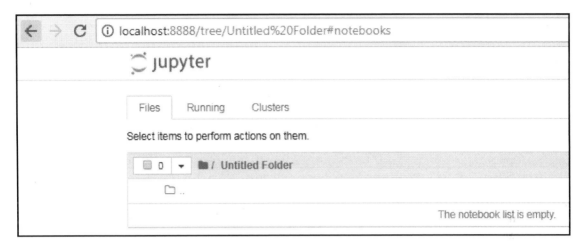

As you can see, it runs out of a web browser, such as Chrome or Firefox, in this case, Chrome. When we begin the Jupyter Notebook, we are in a file browser. We are in a newly created directory called `Untitled Folder`. In Jupyter Notebook there are options for creating new Notebooks, text files, and folders. As seen the the preceding screenshot, currently there is no Notebook saved. We will need a Python Notebook, which can be created by selecting the Python option in the **New** drop-down menu shown in the following screenshot:

When the Notebook has started, we begin with a code block. We can change this code block to a Markdown block, and we can now start entering text.

For example, we can enter a heading. We can also enter plain text along with bold and italics, as shown in the next screenshot:

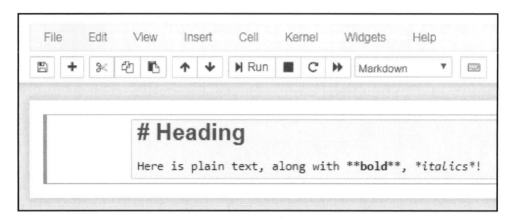

As you can see, there is some hint of how the rendering will look at the end, but we can actually see the rendering by clicking on the run cell button. If we want to change this, we can double-click on the same cell. Now we're back to plain text editing. Here we add monotype and then click on **Run** cell again, shown as follows:

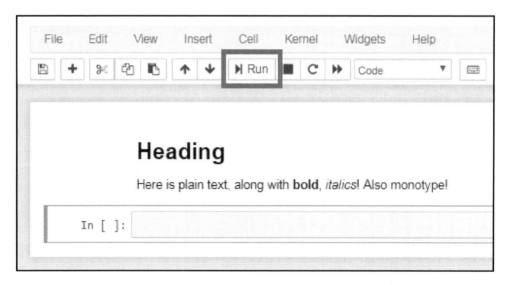

On pressing *Enter*, a new cell is immediately created afterwards. This cell is a Python cell, where we can enter Python code. For example, we can create a variable. We print `Hello, world!` multiple times, as shown in the next screenshot:

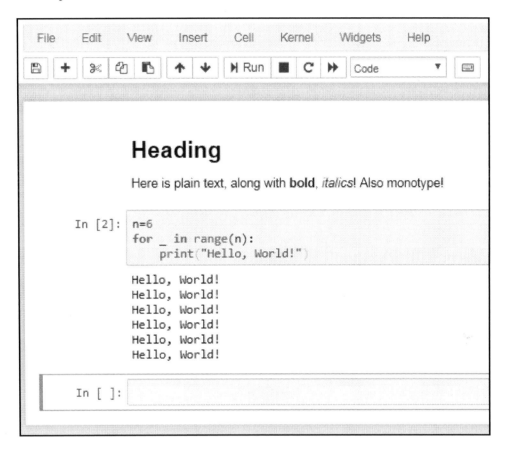

To see what happens when the cell is executed, we simply click on the run cell; also, when we pressed *Enter*, a new cell block was created. Let's make this cell block a Markdown block. If we want to insert an additional cell, we can press **Insert** cell below. In this first cell, we're going to enter some code, and in the second cell, we can enter code that is dependent on code in the first cell. Notice what happens when we try to execute the code in the second cell before executing the code in the first. An error will be produced, shown as follows:

```
In [2]:  n=6
         for _ in range(n):
             print("Hello, World!")

         Hello, World!
         Hello, World!
         Hello, World!
         Hello, World!
         Hello, World!
         Hello, World!

         Now we have multiple cells!

In [3]:  if trigger:
             print("I am triggered!")
         else:
             print("What?")
         ------------------------------------------------------------
         NameError                         Traceback (most recent call last)
         <ipython-input-3-45d8abef433a> in <module>()
         ----> 1 if trigger:
               2     print("I am triggered!")
               3 else:
               4     print("What?")

         NameError: name 'trigger' is not defined

In [ ]:  |
```

The complaint, the variable `trigger`, has not been defined. In order for the second cell to work, we need to run this first cell. Then, when we run the second cell, we get the expected output. Now let's suppose we were to change the code in this cell; say, instead of `trigger = False`, we have `trigger = True`. This second cell will not be aware of the change. If we run this cell again, we get the same output. So we will need to run this cell first, thus affecting the change; then we can run the second cell and get the expected output.

What has happened in the background? What's going on is that there is a kernel, which is basically a running session of Python, tracking all of our variables and everything that has happened up to this point. If we click on **Kernel**, we can see an option to restart the kernel; this will basically restart our session of Python. We are initially warned that by restarting the kernel, all variables will be lost.

When the kernel has been restarted, it doesn't appear as if anything has changed, but if we run the second cell, an error will be produced because the variable `trigger` does not exist. We will need to run the previous cell first in order for this cell to work. If we want to, instead, not merely restart the kernel but restart the kernel and also rerun all cells, we need to click on **Restart & Run All**. After restarting the kernel, all cell blocks will be rerun. It may not appear as if anything has happened, but we have started from the first, run it, run the second cell, and then run the third cell, shown as follows:

```
In [7]:  trigger = True

In [8]:  if trigger:
             print("I am triggered!")
         else:
             print("What?")

         I am triggered!

In [ ]:
```

We can also import libraries. For example, we can import a module from Matplotlib. In this case, in order for Matplotlib to work interactively in a Jupyter Notebook, we will need to use what's called a magic function, which begins with a %, the name of the magic function, and any sort of parameters we need to pass to it. We'll cover these in more detail later, but first let's run that cell block. `plt` has now been loaded, and now we can use it. For example, in this last cell, we will type in the following code:

```
]:  plt.plot([1,2,3,4])
    plt.xlabel("x")
    plt.ylabel("y")
    plt.show()
```

Notice that the output from this cell is inserted directly into the document. We can immediately see the plot that was created. Returning to magic functions, this is not the only function that we have available. Let's see some other functions:

- The magic function, `magic`, will print info about the magic system, as shown in the following screenshot:

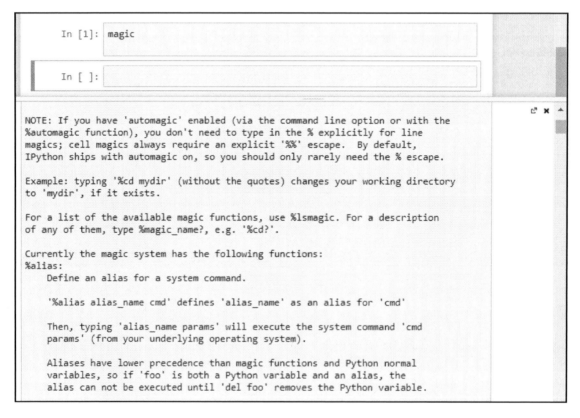

Output of "magic" command

- Another useful function is `timeit`, which we can use to profile code. We first type in `timeit` and then the code that we wish to profile, shown as follows:

```
In [2]: %timeit 2**128
        13 ns ± 0.156 ns per loop (mean ± std. dev. of 7 runs, 100000000 loops each)

In [ ]:
```

- The magic function pwd can be used to see what the working directory is, shown as follows:

```
In [3]: %pwd
Out[3]: 'C:\\Users\\sagarsawant\\Documents'

In [ ]:
```

- The magic function cd can be used to change the working directory, shown as follows:

```
In [4]: %cd D:/Sagar/Documents
        D:\Sagar\Documents

In [ ]:
```

- The magic function pylab is useful if we wish to start both Matplotlib and NumPy in interactive mode, shown as follows:

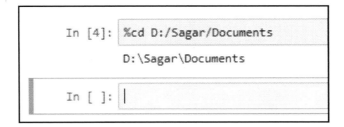

```
In [5]: %pylab
        Using matplotlib backend: Qt5Agg
        Populating the interactive namespace from numpy and matplotlib

In [ ]:
```

If we wish to see a list of available magic functions, we can type `lsmagic`, shown as follows:

```
In [6]:  %lsmagic

Out[6]:  Available line magics:
         %alias  %alias_magic  %autocall  %automagic  %autosave  %bookmark  %cd  %clear  %cls  %colors  %config  %connect_info  %copy  %d
         dir  %debug  %dhist  %dirs  %doctest_mode  %echo  %ed  %edit  %env  %gui  %hist  %history  %killbgscripts  %ldir  %less  %load
         %load_ext  %loadpy  %logoff  %logon  %logstart  %logstate  %logstop  %ls  %lsmagic  %macro  %magic  %matplotlib  %mkdir  %more
         %notebook  %page  %pastebin  %pdb  %pdef  %pdoc  %pfile  %pinfo  %pinfo2  %popd  %pprint  %precision  %profile  %prun  %psearch
         %psource  %pushd  %pwd  %pycat  %pylab  %qtconsole  %quickref  %recall  %rehashx  %reload_ext  %ren  %rep  %rerun  %reset  %rese
         t_selective  %rmdir  %run  %save  %sc  %set_env  %store  %sx  %system  %tb  %time  %timeit  %unalias  %unload_ext  %who  %who_ls
         %whos  %xdel  %xmode

         Available cell magics:
         %%!  %%HTML  %%SVG  %%bash  %%capture  %%cmd  %%debug  %%file  %%html  %%javascript  %%js  %%latex  %%markdown  %%perl  %%prun
         %%pypy  %%python  %%python2  %%python3  %%ruby  %%script  %%sh  %%svg  %%sx  %%system  %%time  %%timeit  %%writefile

         Automagic is ON, % prefix IS NOT needed for line magics.

In [ ]:  |
```

And if we wish for a quick reference sheet, we can use the magic function `quickref`, shown as follows:

```
IPython -- An enhanced Interactive Python - Quick Reference Card
================================================================

obj?, obj??     : Get help, or more help for object (also works as
                  ?obj, ??obj).
?foo.*abc*      : List names in 'foo' containing 'abc' in them.
%magic          : Information about IPython's 'magic' % functions.

Magic functions are prefixed by % or %%, and typically take their arguments
without parentheses, quotes or even commas for convenience.  Line magics take a
single % and cell magics are prefixed with two %%.

Example magic function calls:

%alias d ls -F  : 'd' is now an alias for 'ls -F'
alias d ls -F   : Works if 'alias' not a python name
alist = %alias  : Get list of aliases to 'alist'
cd /usr/share   : Obvious. cd -<tab> to choose from visited dirs.
%cd??           : See help AND source for magic %cd
%timeit x=10    : time the 'x=10' statement with high precision.
%%timeit x=2**100
x**100          : time 'x**100' with a setup of 'x=2**100'; setup code is not
                  counted.  This is an example of a cell magic.
```

Now that we're done with this Notebook, let's give it a name. Let's simply call it My Notebook. This is done by clicking on the name of the Notebook at the top of the editor pane. Finally, you can save, and after saving, you can close and halt the Notebook. So this will close the Notebook and halt the Notebook's kernel. That would be the clean way to leave the Notebook. Notice now, in our tree, we can see the directory where the Notebook was saved, and we can see that the Notebook exists in that directory. It is an ipynb document.

Exploring alternatives to Jupyter

Now we will consider alternatives to Jupyter Notebooks. We will look at:

- Jupyter QT Console
- Spyder
- Rodeo
- Python interpreter
- ptpython

The first alternative we will consider is the Jupyter QT Console; this is a Python interpreter with added functionality, aimed specifically for data analysis.

The following screenshot shows the Jupyter QT Console:

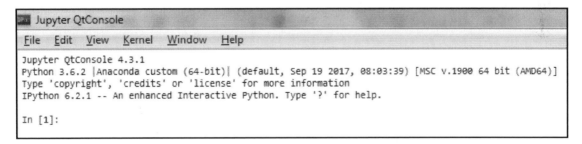

It is very similar to the Jupyter Notebook. In fact, it is effectively the Console version of the Jupyter Notebook. Notice here that we have some interesting syntax. We have `In [1]`, and then let's suppose you were to type in a command, for example:

```
print ("Hello, world!")
```

```
Jupyter QtConsole 4.3.1
Python 3.6.2 |Anaconda custom (64-bit)| (default, Sep 19 2017, 08:03:39) [MSC v.1900 64 bit (AMD64)]
Type 'copyright', 'credits' or 'license' for more information
IPython 6.2.1 -- An enhanced Interactive Python. Type '?' for help.

In [1]: print ("Hello, world!")
Hello, world!
```

We see some output and then we see `In [2]`.

Now let's try something else:

```
1 + 1
```

```
In [2]: 1 + 1
Out[2]: 2
```

Right after `In [2]`, we see `Out[2]`. What does this mean? This is a way to track historical commands and their outputs in a session. To access, say, the command for `In [42]`, we type `_i42`. So, in this case, if we want to see the input for command 2, we type in `i2`. Notice that it gives us a string, 1 + 1. In fact, we can run this string.

If we type in `eval` and then `_i2`, notice that it gives us the same output as the original command, `In [2]`, did. Now, how about `Out[2]`? How can we access the actual output? In this case, all we would do is just `_` and then the number of the output, say 2. This should give us 2. So this gives you a more convenient way to access historical commands and their outputs.

Another advantage of Jupyter Notebooks is that you can see images. For example, let's get Matplotlib running. First we're going to import Matplotlib with the following command:

```
import matplotlib.pyplot as plt
```

After we've imported Matplotlib, recall that we need to run a certain magic, the Matplotlib magic:

```
%matplotlib inline
```

We need to give it the inline parameter, and now we can create a Matplotlib figure. Notice that the image shows up right below the command. When we type in _8, it shows that a Matplotlib object was created, but it does not actually show the plot itself. As you can see, we can use the Jupyter console in a more advanced way than the typical Python console. For example, let's work with a dataset called `Iris`; import it using the following line:

```
from sklearn.datasets import load_iris
```

This is a very common dataset used in data analysis. It's often used as a way to evaluate training models. We will also use k-means clustering on this:

```
from sklearn.cluster import KMeans
```

The `load_Iris` function isn't actually the `Iris` dataset; it is a function that we can use to get the `Iris` dataset. The following command will actually give us access to that dataset:

```
iris  = load_iris()
```

Now we will train a k-means clustering scheme on this dataset:

```
iris_clusters = KMeans(n_clusters = 3, init =  "random").fit(iris.data)
```

We can see the documentation right away when we're typing in a function. For example, I know what the end clusters parameter means; it is actually the original doc string from the function. Here, I want the number of clusters to be 3, because I know that there are actually three real clusters in this dataset. Now that a clustering scheme has been trained, we can plot it using the following code:

```
plt.scatter(iris.data[:, 0], iris.data[:, 1], c = iris_clusters.labels_)
```

Spyder

Spyder is an IDE unlike the Jupyter Notebook or the Jupyter QT Console. It integrates NumPy, SciPy, Matplotlib, and IPython. It is extensible with plugins, and it is included with Anaconda.

The following screenshot shows Spyder, an actual IDE intended for data analysis and scientific computing:

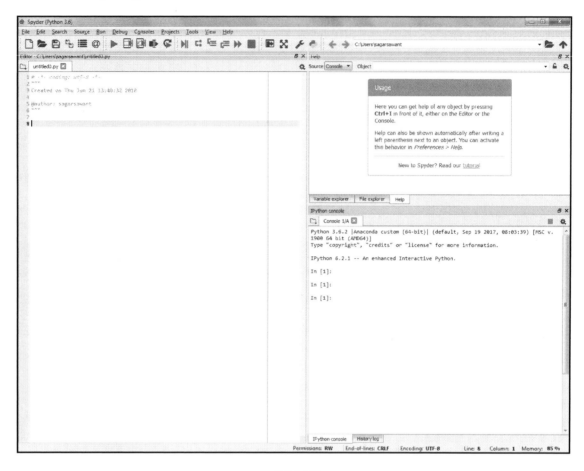

Spyder Python 3.6

On the right, you can go to File explorer to search for new files to load. Here, we want to open up `iris_kmeans.py`. This is a file that contains all the commands that we used before in the Jupyter QT Console. Notice on the right that the editor has a console; that is in fact the IPython console, which you saw as the Jupyter QT Console. We can run this entire file by clicking on the **Run** tab. It will run in the console, shown as follows:

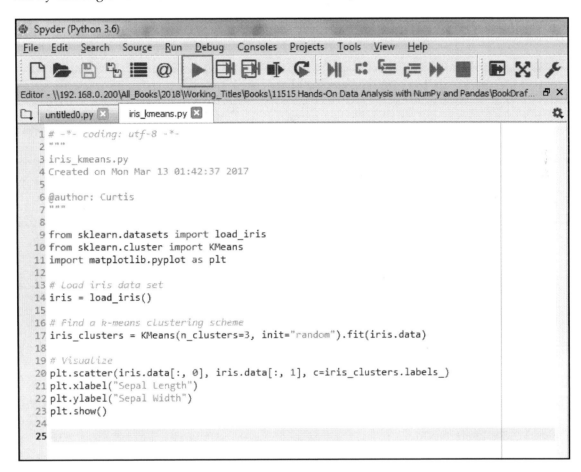

The following screenshot will be the output:

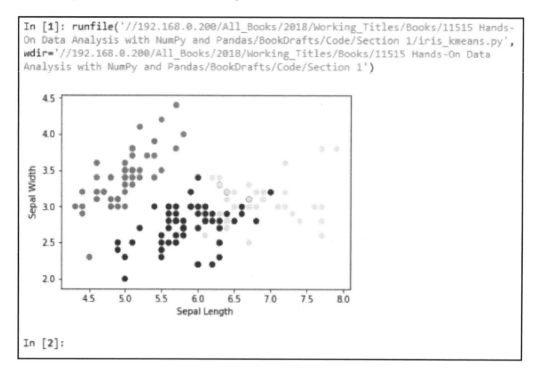

Notice that at the end we see the result of the clustering that we saw before. We can type in commands interactively as well; for example, we can make our computer say `Hello, world!`.

In the editor, let's type in a new variable, let's say n = 5. Now let's run this file in the editor. Notice that n is a variable that the editor is aware of. Now let's make a change, say n = 6. Unless we were to actually run this file again, the console will be unaware of the change. So if I were to type n in the console again, nothing changes, and it's still 5. You would need to run this line in order to actually see a change.

We also have a variable explorer where we can see the values of variables and change them. For example, I can change the value of n from 6 to 10, shown as follows:

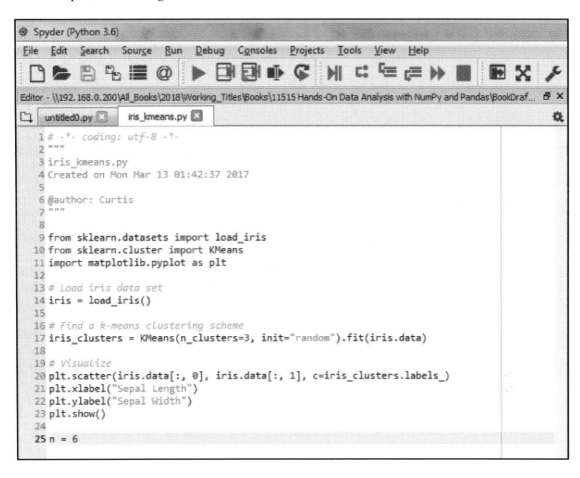

The following screenshot shows the output:

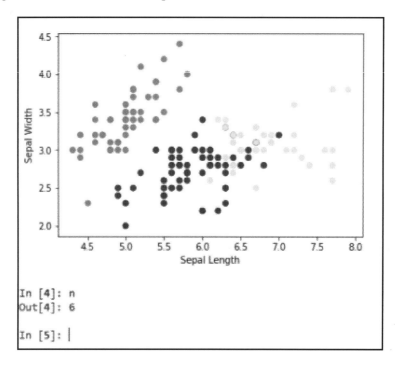

Then, when I go to the console and ask what n is, it will say 10:

```
n
10
```

That concludes our discussion of Spyder.

Rodeo

Rodeo is a Python IDE developed by Yhat, and is intended for data analysis applications exclusively. It is intended to emulate the RStudio IDE, which is popular among R users, and it can be downloaded from Rodeo's website. The only advantage of the base Python interpreter is that every Python installation includes it, shown as follows:

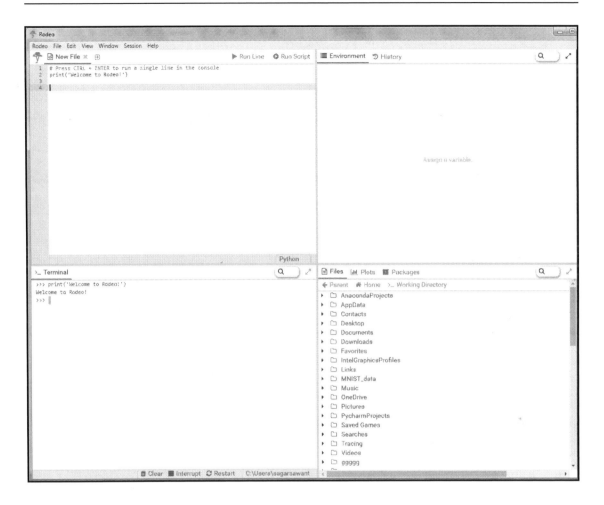

ptpython

What may be a lesser known console-based Python REPL is `ptpython`, designed by
Jonathan Slenders. It exists only in the console and is an independent project by him. You
can find it on GitHub. It has lightweight features, yet it also includes syntax highlighting,
autocompletion, and even IPython. It can be installed with the following command:

```
pip install ptpython
```

That concludes our discussion on alternatives to the Jupyter Notebooks.

Package management with Conda

We will now discuss package management with Conda. In this section, we're going to take a look at the following topics:

- What is Conda?
- Managing Conda environments
- Managing Python with Conda
- Managing packages with Conda

What is Conda?

So what is Conda? Conda is the Anaconda package manager. Conda allows us to create and manage multiple environments, allowing multiple versions of Python, R, and their relevant packages to exist. This can be very useful if you need to develop for different systems with different versions of Python and their packages. Conda allows you to manage Python and R versions, and it also facilitates installation and management of packages.

Conda environment management

A Conda environment allows developers to use and manage different versions of Python in its packages. This can be useful for testing and development on legacy systems. Environments can be saved, cloned, and exported so that others can replicate results.

Here are some common environment management commands.

For environment creation:

```
conda create --name env_name prog1 prog2
conda create --name env_name python=3 prog3
```

For listing environments:

```
conda env list
```

To verify the environment:

```
conda info --envs
```

To clone the environment:

```
conda create --name new_env --clone old_env
```

To remove environments:

```
conda remove --name env_name -all
```

Users can share environments by creating a YAML file, which recipients can use to construct an identical environment. You can do this by hand, where you effectively replicate what Anaconda would make, but it is much easier to have Anaconda create a YAML file for you.

After you have created such a file, or if you've received this file from another user, it is very easy to create a new environment.

Managing Python

As mentioned earlier, Anaconda allows you to manage multiple versions of Python. It is possible to search and see which versions of Python are available for installation. You can verify which version of Python is in an environment, and you can even create environments for Python 2.7. You can also update the version of Python that is in a current environment.

Package management

Let's suppose that we're interested in installing the package selenium, which is a package that is used for web scraping and also web testing. We can list the packages that are currently installed, and we can give the command to install a new package.

First, we should search to see whether the package is available from the Conda system. Not all packages that are available on pip are available from Conda. That said, it is in fact possible to install a package available from pip, although hopefully, if we wish to install a package, we can use the following command:

```
conda install selenium
```

If selenium is the package we're interested in, it can be downloaded automatically from the internet, unless you have a file that Anaconda can install directly from your system.

To install packages via `pip`, use the following:

```
pip install package_name
```

Packages, of course, can be removed as follows:

```
conda remove selenium
```

Setting up a database

We'll now begin discussing setting up a database for you to use. In this section, we're going to look at the following topics:

- Installing MySQL
- Installing MySQL connector for Python
- Creating, using, and deleting databases

MySQL connector is necessary in order to use MySQL with Python. There are many SQL database implementations in existence, and while MySQL may not be the simplest database management system, it is full-featured, it is industrial-strength, it is commonly seen in real world situations, and furthermore, it is free and open source, which means it's an excellent tool to learn on. You can obtain the MySQL Community Edition, which is the free and open source version, from MySQL's website (go to `https://dev.mysql.com/downloads/`).

Installing MySQL

For Linux systems, if it's possible, I recommend that you install MySQL using whatever package management system is available to you. Perhaps go for YUM, if you're using a Red-Hat-based distribution, APT if you're using a Debian-based distro, or SUSE's repository system. If you do not have a package management system, you may need to install MySQL from the source.

Windows users can install MySQL directly from their website. You should also be aware that MySQL comes in 32-bit and 64-bit binaries, but whatever program you download will likely install the correct version for your system.

Here is the web page from where you can download MySQL for Windows:

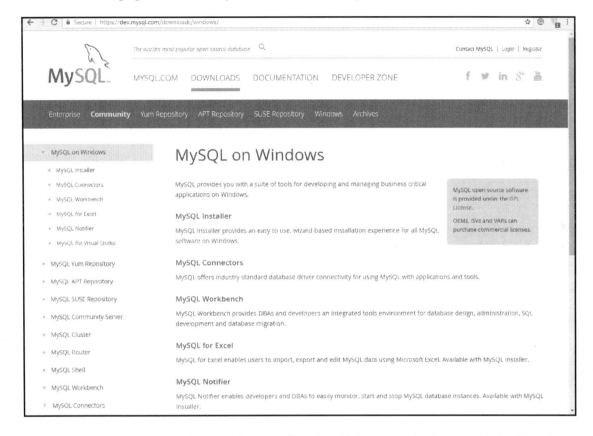

I recommend that you use the MySQL Installer. Scroll down, and when you're looking for which binary to download, be aware that this first binary says web community. This is going to be an installer that downloads MySQL from the internet as you're doing the installation. Notice that it's much smaller than the other binary. It basically includes everything you need in order to be able to install MySQL. This would be the one I would recommend you download if you're following along.

There are generally available releases; these should be stable. Next to the generally available releases tab are the development releases; I recommend that you do not download these unless you know what you're doing.

MySQL connectors

MySQL functions like a driver on your system, and other applications interact with MySQL as if it were a driver. So, you will need to download a MySQL connector in order to be able to use MySQL with Python. This will allow Python to communicate with MySQL. What you will end up doing is loading in a package, and you will start up a connection with MySQL. The Python connector can be downloaded from MySQL's website (go to `https://dev.mysql.com/downloads/connector/`).

This web page is universal for any operating system, so you will need to select the appropriate platform, such as Linux, OS X, or Windows. You'll need to select and download the installer best matching the system's architecture, whether you have a 32-bit or 64-bit, and the version of Python. And then you will use the install wizard in order to install it on your system.

Here is the page for downloading and installing the connector:

Notice that we can choose here which platform is appropriate. We even have platform-independent and source code versions. It may also be possible to install this using a package management system, such as APT if you're using a Debian-based system, Ubuntu or YUM if you're using a Red-Hat-based system, and so on. We have many different installers, so we will need to be aware which version of Python we're using. It is recommended that you use the version that is closest to the one that is actually being used in your project. You'll also need to choose between 32-bit and 64-bit. Then you click on download and follow the instructions of the installer.

So, database management is a major topic; to go into everything about database management would take us well beyond the scope of this book. We're not going to talk about how a good database is designed; I recommend that you go to another resource, perhaps another Packt product that would explain these topics, because they are important. Regarding SQL, we will tell you only the commands that you need to use SQL at a basic level. There's also no discussion on permissions, so we're going to assume that your database gives full permission to whichever user is using it, and there's only one user at a time.

Creating a database

After installing MySQL in the MySQL command line, we can create a database with the following command, with the name of the database after it:

```
create database
```

Every command must be ended by a semicolon; otherwise, MySQL will wait until the command is actually finished.

You can see all available databases with this command:

```
show databases
```

We can specify which database we want to use with the following command:

```
use database_name
```

If we wish to delete a database, we can do so with the following command:

```
drop database database_name
```

Here is the MySQL command line:

Let's practice managing databases. We can create a database with the following command:

```
create database mydb
```

To see all databases, we can use this command:

```
show databases
```

There are multiple databases here, some of which are from other projects, but as you can see, the database `mydb`, which we just created, is shown as follows:

If we want to use this database, the command `use mydb` can be used. MySQL says the database has been changed. What this means is that when I issue commands such as creating tables, reading from tables, or adding new data, all of this will be done with the database `mydb`.

Let's say we want to delete the database `mydb`; we can do so with the following command:

```
drop database mydb
```

This will delete the database.

Summary

In this chapter, we were introduced to Anaconda, learned why it is a useful starting point, downloaded it, and installed it. We explored some alternatives to Jupyter, covered managing the Anaconda package, and also learned how to set up a MySQL database. Nevertheless, throughout the rest of the book, we'll presume Anaconda has been installed. In the next chapter, we will talk about using NumPy, a useful package in data analysis. Without this package, data analysis with Python would be all but impossible.

Diving into NumPY

By now you should have installed everything you need to use Python for data analysis. Let's now begin discussing NumPy, an important package for managing data and performing calculations. Without NumPy, there would not be any data analysis using Python, so understanding NumPy is critical. Our key objective in this chapter is learning to use the tools provided in NumPy.

In this chapter, the following topics will be covered:

- NumPy data types
- Creating arrays
- Slicing arrays
- Mathematics
- Methods and functions

We begin by discussing data types, which are conceptually important when handling NumPy arrays. In this chapter, we will discuss NumPy data types controlled by `dtype` objects, which are the way NumPy stores and manages data. We'll also briefly introduce NumPy arrays called `ndarray` and discuss what they do.

NumPy arrays

Let's now talk about NumPy arrays, which are called `ndarray`. These are not the arrays you may encounter in C or C++. A better analog is matrices in MATLAB or R; that is, they behave like a mathematical object resembling a mathematical vector, matrix, or tensor. While they can store non-mathematical information such as strings, they exist mainly to manage and facilitate operations with data that is numeric in nature. `ndarray` are assigned a particular data type or `dtype` upon creation, and all current and future data in the array must be of that `dtype`. They also have more than one-dimension, referred to as **axes**.

A one-dimensional ndarray is a line of data; this would be a vector. A two-dimensional ndarray would be a square of data, effectively a matrix. A three-dimensional ndarray would be key book data, like a tensor. Any number of dimensions is permitted, but most ndarray are one or two-dimensional.

dtype are similar to types in the basic Python language, but NumPy dtype resemble the data types seen in other languages too, such as C, C++, or Fortran, in that they are of fixed length. dtype do have a hierarchy; a dtype usually has a string descriptor, followed by a power of 2 that determines how large the dtype is.

Here is a list of common dtype:

Type	Description
int8, int16, int32, int64	Integer (signed)
uint8, uint16, uint32, uint64	Integer (unsigned)
float16, float32, float64, float128	Floating-point number
bool_	Boolean (True or False)
string_	Fixed-length string type
unicode_	Fixed-length unicode type

Let's see some of the stuff that we just discussed in action. The first thing we're going to do is load in the NumPy library. Next, we will create an array of 1s, and they're going to be integers.

This is what the array looks like:

```
In [2]:  # Creating arrays of ones, but with differing dtypes
         int_ones = np.ones((2, 2), dtype = np.int8)
         int_ones

Out[2]:  array([[1, 1],
                [1, 1]], dtype=int8)
```

If we look at the dtype, we see it is int8, in other words, 8-bit integers. We can also create an array filled with 16-bit floating-point numbers. This array looks similar to the array of integers. There is a dot at the end of the 1s; that's somewhat of an indicator that the data contained is floating-point rather than integer.

Let's create an array filled with unsigned integers:

```
In [6]:  uint_ones = np.ones((2, 2), dtype = np.uint8)
         uint_ones

Out[6]:  array([[1, 1],
                [1, 1]], dtype=uint8)
```

Again, they're 1s and it looks similar to what we have before, but now let's try to change some of the data. For example, we can change a number to -1 in the array int_ones and it's fine. But if I try to change it to -1 in the unsigned integers, I will end up with 255.

Let's create an array filled with strings:

```
In [11]:  string_arr = np.array(["Sam", "Bill", "Gary"])
          string_arr

Out[11]:  array(['Sam', 'Bill', 'Gary'],
                dtype='<U4')
```

We haven't specified the dtype argument here, because usually the dtype is guessed; a good guess is usually made, but there's no guarantee. For example, here I want to assign a new value of Waldo to the contents of this array. Now, this dtype means that you have strings that cannot exceed a length of four. Waldo has five characters though, so when we change the array and change its contents, we end up with Wald rather than Waldo. This is because it can't have more than five characters; it just takes the first four:

```
In [12]:  string_arr[1] = "Waldo"
          string_arr     # Cannot have strings longer than 4 characters

Out[12]:  array(['Sam', 'Wald', 'Gary'],
                dtype='<U4')
```

I could specify the dtype manually and say that 16 characters are allowed; in this case, Waldo works fine.

Special numeric values

In addition to `dtype` objects, NumPy introduces special numeric values: `nan` and `inf`. These can arise in mathematical computations. **Not A Number (nan)**. It indicates that a value that should be numeric is, in fact, not defined mathematically. For example, `0/0` yields `nan`. Sometimes, `nan` is also used to signify missing information; for example, pandas uses this. `inf` indicates a quantity that is arbitrarily large, so in practice, it means larger than any number the computer can conceive of. `-inf` is also defined and it means arbitrarily small. This could occur if a numeric operation blows up, that is, grows rapidly without bounds.

Nothing is ever equal to `nan`; it makes no sense for something undefined to be equal to something else. You need to use the NumPy function `isnan` to identify `nan`. While the `==` sign does not work for `nan`, it does work for `inf`. That said, you're better off distinguishing finite and infinite values using the function is finite or is `inf`. Arithmetic involving `nan` and `inf` is defined, but be warned that it may not get you what you want. Some special functions are defined to help avoid issues when `nan` or `inf` is present. For example, `nan` sum computes sums of iterable objects while omitting `nan`. You can find a full list of such functions in the NumPy documentation. I will mention them only when I use them.

Let's now work on an example:

1. First, we will create an array and it's going to be filled with 1, −1, and 0. Then, we divide this by 0 and see what we get. So, the moment we do this, it complains, because obviously we're not supposed to divide by 0. We learned this in elementary school!

```
In [17]:  vec1 = np.array([1, -1, 0], dtype=np.float16)
          vec2 = vec1 / 0
          vec2

          C:\Anaconda3\lib\site-packages\ipykernel\__main__.py:2: RuntimeWarning: divide by zero encountered in true_divide
            from ipykernel import kernelapp as app
          C:\Anaconda3\lib\site-packages\ipykernel\__main__.py:2: RuntimeWarning: invalid value encountered in true_divide
            from ipykernel import kernelapp as app
Out[17]:  array([ inf, -inf,  nan], dtype=float16)
```

That said, it does come up with numbers: `1/0` is `inf`, `−1/0` is `−inf`, and `0/0` is not a number. So how can we detect special values?

2. Let's first run a loop that is wrong:

```
In [18]:   # Can we detect special values?
           for i in vec2:
               print(i)
               print('------')
               print('Inf: ' + str(i == np.inf))
               print('-Inf: ' + str(i == -np.inf))
               print('NaN: ' + str(i == np.nan))     # Doesn't work!
               print('\n\n')

           inf
           ------
           Inf: True
           -Inf: False
           NaN: False



           -inf
           ------
           Inf: False
           -Inf: True
           NaN: False



           nan
           ------
           Inf: False
           -Inf: False
           NaN: False
```

We're going to iterate through every possible value of vec2 and print the results of `i == np.inf, i == -np.inf`, and whether I is equal to nan, `i == np.nan`. What we get is a list; the first two blocks of `inf` and `-inf` are fine, but this nan is not fine. We wanted it to detect a nan but it did not do so. So, let's try it using the is nan function:

```
In [19]:  # A better way
          for i in vec2:
              print(i)
              print('------')
              print('Inf:  ' + str(i == np.inf))
              print('-Inf: ' + str(i == -np.inf))
              print('NaN:  ' + str(np.isnan(i)))     # Does work!
              print('\n\n')

inf
------
Inf: True
-Inf: False
NaN: False



-inf
------
Inf: False
-Inf: True
NaN: False



nan
------
Inf: False
-Inf: False
NaN: True
```

This does in fact work; we were able to detect the nan.

3. Now, let's detect finite versus infinite:

```
In [20]: # Finite vs. infinite
         for i in vec2:
             print(i)
             print('------')
             print('Is finite?: ' + str(np.isfinite(i)))
             print('Is infinite?: ' + str(np.isinf(i)))
             print('\n\n')

inf
------
Is finite?: False
Is infinite?: True



-inf
------
Is finite?: False
Is infinite?: True



nan
------
Is finite?: False
Is infinite?: False
```

Not surprisingly, `inf` is not finite. Neither is `-inf`. But `nan` counts as neither finite or infinite; it is undefined. Let's see what happens when we do `inf + 1`, and `inf * -1`, and `nan + 1`. We always get `nan`.

If we raise 2 to the power of negative infinity, what we get is 0. But if we raise it to infinity, we get infinity. And `inf - inf` is not equal to any specific number:

```
In [24]: 2 ** vec2[1]
Out[24]: 0.0

In [25]: 2 ** vec2[0]
Out[25]: inf

In [26]: np.inf - np.inf
Out[26]: nan
```

4. Now, let's create an array and fill it with a number, 999. If we were to raise this array to itself, in other words, 999 to the power of 999, what we end up with is inf:

```
In [27]: vec3 = np.array([999], dtype=np.float64)
         vec3
Out[27]: array([ 999.])

In [28]: vec3[0] ** vec3[0]    # Huge; gives inf, even though this is finite
         C:\Anaconda3\lib\site-packages\ipykernel\__main__.py:1: RuntimeWarning: overflow encountered in double_scalars
           if __name__ == '__main__':
Out[28]: inf
```

This is too large a number for these programs to handle. That said, we know that this number is not actually infinite. It is finite, but to the computer it is so large that it may as well be infinite.

5. Now, let's create an array and give the first element of this array as nan. If we sum up the elements of this array, what we get is nan because nan + anything is nan:

```
In [29]: vec4 = np.ones(5)
         vec4[0] = np.nan
         vec4
Out[29]: array([ nan,    1.,    1.,    1.,    1.])

In [30]: np.sum(vec4)
Out[30]: nan

In [31]: np.nansum(vec4)    # Ignores nans
Out[31]: 4.0
```

But, if we use the function nansum, the nans will be ignored and we'll get a reasonable value of 4.

Creating NumPy arrays

Now that we have discussed NumPy data types and have been briefly introduced to NumPy arrays, let's talk about how we can create NumPy arrays. In this section, we will create NumPy arrays using various functions. There are functions that create what are known as empty `ndarray`; functions for creating `ndarray` filled with 0s, 1s, or random numbers; and functions for creating `ndarray` using data. We will discuss all of these, along with saving and loading NumPy arrays from disk. There are a few ways to create arrays. One way is to use the array function, where we give an iterable object or a list of iterable objects, from which an array will be generated.

We will do this using lists of lists, but these could be lists of tuples, tuples of tuples, or even other arrays. There are ways to automatically create arrays filled with data as well. For example, we can use functions such as `ones`, `zeros`, or `randn`; the latter is filled with randomly generated data. These arrays require passing a tuple that determines the shape of an array, that is, how many dimensions the array has and how long each dimension is. Each creates arrays that are considered empty, containing no data of interest. This is usually garbage data that is made up of whatever bits were in the memory location where the array was created.

We can specify the `dtype` parameter if we want, but if we do not, the `dtype` will either be guessed or floating-point. Notice the last line in the following table:

Creation Method	Description
array(arr, dtype)	Generates an array based on arr with specified dtype (optional; if not specified, best guess)
ones(shape, dtype) zeros(shape, dtype)	Generates an array filled with ones/zeros of specified shape (using a tuple) with specified dtype (floating point by default)
empty(shape, dtype)	Like ones/zeros, but filled with "garbage" data
ndarray(shape, dtype)	Like empty()
randn(shape)	An array filled with Normally-distributed random numbers (floating point by default), with specified shape
arr2 = arr1.copy()	Copies the contents of arr1 into a new array, arr2

It's a mistake to think that you can copy an `arr1` by assigning it to a new variable. Instead, what you effectively get is a new pointer to the same data. If you want a new array with the same data that is completely independent of its parent, you will need to use the `copy` method, as we will see.

Creating ndarray

In the following notebook, we create an `ndarray`. The first thing we're going to do is create a vector of 1s. Notice the tuple that is being passed; it contains only one number, 5. Therefore, it will be a one-dimensional `ndarray` with five elements:

```
In [1]:  # A common idiom for importing NumPy
         # (Could also use pylab, which imports all NumPy functions into global namespace)
         import numpy as np

         vec1 = np.ones((5))

         print(vec1)
         [ 1.  1.  1.  1.  1.]
```

It was automatically assigned the `dtype` floating-point 64:

```
In [2]:  vec1.dtype

Out[2]:  dtype('float64')
```

If we want to convert this to an integer, we can attempt to do it the following way first, but the result will be garbage:

```
In [3]:  vec1.dtype = np.int8
         print(vec1)
         vec1.dtype

         [  0   0   0   0   0   0 -16  63   0   0   0   0   0   0 -16  63   0   0
            0   0   0   0 -16  63   0   0   0   0   0   0 -16  63   0   0   0   0
            0   0 -16  63]

Out[3]:  dtype('int8')
```

You need to be very careful when you're converting a `dtype`.

The correct way to do this is to first create an original vector consisting of five 1s, and then create a brand new array using those elements as the input. The following is the result:

```
In [4]: vec1 = np.ones((5))
        vec1 = np.array(vec1, dtype = np.int8)
        print(vec1)

        [1 1 1 1 1]

In [5]: print(vec1.dtype)

        int8
```

Notice that `vec1`, in fact, has the correct data type. We could, of course, have circumvented this by specifying the `dtype` that we wanted initially. In this case, we wanted 8-bit integers. This is the result:

```
In [6]: vec1 = np.ones((5), dtype=np.int8)
        vec1.dtype

Out[6]: dtype('int8')

In [7]: print(vec1)

        [1 1 1 1 1]
```

Now, let's make a cube of 0s. Here, we're going to create an array that'll be three-dimensional; that is, we have rows, we have columns, and we have slabs.

So, we have two rows, two columns, and two slabs, in that order, and we're going to make this into 64-bit floating-point numbers. Here is the result:

```
In [8]: arr1 = np.zeros((2, 2, 2), dtype=np.float64)
        print(arr1)

        [[[ 0.  0.]
          [ 0.  0.]]

         [[ 0.  0.]
          [ 0.  0.]]]
```

The top part in the result will be considered one slab, and the bottom part will be considered the other slab.

Now let's create a matrix filled with random data. In this case, we're going to have a square matrix with three rows and three columns, created using the `randn` function, which is a part of the random module of NumPy:

```
In [9]:  mat1 = np.random.randn(3, 3)
         print(mat1)

         [[-0.28118485 -1.90090082  1.07767092]
          [ 1.43841178 -1.66880004  0.33062882]
          [-0.93944768  1.17388981  0.78395216]]
```

 The first number that we pass is the number of rows, and the second number is the number of columns. You could have passed a third number that will determine the number of slabs, and a fourth, a fifth, and so on to specify the number of dimensions you want, and how long you want each dimension to be.

Now we're going to create 2 x 2 matrices with names that we've chosen, and 2 x 2 x 2 arrays containing numbers. So here is a matrix containing just names:

```
In [10]:  mat2 = np.array([["bob", "jane"], ["bill", "janet"]])
          print(mat2)

          [['bob' 'jane']
           ['bill' 'janet']]

In [11]:  mat2.dtype

Out[11]:  dtype('<U5')
```

And we can see that `dtype` is `U5`, that is, five-letter-long Unicode strings.

We can also use tuples to create our arrays:

```
In [13]:  # Tuples can be used too
          arr2 = np.array([[(1, 3, 5), (2, 4, 6)], [(1, np.nan, 1), (2, 2, 2)]])
          # Despite the integers, nan forces the array to hold floats
          print(arr2)
```

In this case, we have an array with multiple levels, so this is going to end up being a three-dimensional array. (1, 3, 5) is going to be the first row of the first slab of this array, and (2, 4, 6) will be the second row of the first slab. [(1, 3, 5), (2, 4, 6)] determines the first slab. [(1, np.nan, 1), (2, 2, 2)] determines the second slab. In all, we end up with a cube of data:

```
In [13]:   # Tuples can be used too
           arr2 = np.array([[(1, 3, 5), (2, 4, 6)], [(1, np.nan, 1), (2, 2, 2)]])
           # Despite the integers, nan forces the array to hold floats
           print(arr2)

           [[[ 1.   3.   5.]
             [ 2.   4.   6.]]

            [[ 1.   nan   1.]
             [ 2.   2.   2.]]]

           Let's say I want to copy mat2. Here's the first attempt:
```

As we covered earlier, if we wish to copy the contents of an array, we need to be careful.

Consider the following example:

```
In [13]:   mat2_cpy = mat2
           print(mat2_cpy)

           [['bob' 'jane']
            ['bill' 'janet']]
```

For example, we might think naively that this will create a new copy of mat2, storing it in mat2_copy. But watch what happens if we were to change an entry in the supposed copy of this array, or change an entry of the original parent array. In mat2, if we change the element in the first row and the first column (that is element *(0,0)*) to liam, this is the result:

```
In [14]:   mat2[0,0] = 'liam'
           print(mat2)

           [['liam' 'jane']
            ['bill' 'janet']]
```

If we look at the copy, we will notice that the change has affected the copy as well:

```
In [17]:   print(mat2_cpy)

           [['liam' 'jane']
            ['bill' 'janet']]
```

So if we want an independent copy, we need to use the `copy` method. Then, when we change the 0,0 element of `mat2`, it does not affect the `copy` method:

```
In [16]:   mat2_cpy = mat2.copy()
           mat2[0,0] = "amy"
           print(mat2)

           [['amy' 'jane']
            ['bill' 'janet']]
```

We can also make changes to the copy and it will not affect the parent.

Here is a list of common ways to save `ndarray` objects:

Save Method	Description
save(file, arr)	Saves arr in file in .npy format
savez(file, arr1, arr2, ...) savez_compressed(file, arr1, ...)	Saves arr1, arr2, and other arrays in file as .npz format (use savez_compressed() for a compressed file)
savetxt(file, arr, delimiter)	Saves arr in file, a text file; optional argument delimiter gives string or character separating columns (so use delimiter=',' for a CSV file)
arr.tofile(file, sep)	arr is saved to file (either an open file object or a filename), with array items separated by sep; if sep="", this will be a binary file (text otherwise)

You is recommended to use the `save`, `savez`, or `savetxt` functions. I've shown the common syntax for these functions in the preceding table. In the case of `savetxt`, if you want a comma-separated file, simply set the delimiter argument to the comma character. Also, `savetxt` can save a compressed text file if the name of the file ends with `.gz`, thus saving a step as you don't need to compress the text file yourself later. Be aware that, unless you write a full file path, the file specified will be saved in the working directory.

Let's see how we might be able to save some arrays. The first thing that we should probably do is check what our working directory is:

```
In [20]:  %pwd

Out[20]:  'C:\\Users\\sagarsawant\\Documents\\New folder (2)'
```

Now in this case, I am automatically in the working directory that I want. But if I wished, I could change the working directory with the `cd` command, and then I would, in fact, have that directory as my working directory:

```
In [20]:  %cd "D:\Curtis\Documents\Jupyter Notebooks"

          D:\Curtis\Documents\Jupyter Notebooks
```

That said, let's create an `npy` file, which is a native file format for NumPy. We can save the array in this file format using the `save` function from NumPy:

```
In [22]:  np.save("arr1", arr1)
```

This is a binary file now in our working directory. We can load the array in this file using `load()`.

What we will have is an `npy` file named `arr1`. This is, in fact, a binary file in our working directory.

If we wish to load the array that is saved in this file, we can do so using the `load` function:

```
In [22]:  arr1_new = np.load("arr1.npy")
          print(arr1_new)

          [[[ 0.  0.]
            [ 0.  0.]]

           [[ 0.  0.]
            [ 0.  0.]]]

          Let's create a CSV file that holds the information in  mat1 .
```

We can also create a CSV file that holds the same information in mat1. For example, we can save it with the following function:

```
In [23]:  np.savetxt("mat1.csv", mat1, delimiter=",")

          Let's preview what the contents of  mat1.csv  look like.
```

We can see what the contents of mat1.csv look like using this code:

```
In [25]:  mat1file = open("mat1.csv", "r")
          for l in mat1file:
              print(l)

          -2.811848548885137467e-01,-1.900900816747193467e+00,1.077670922205850257e+00

          1.438411778539517183e+00,-1.668800040929424799e+00,3.306288224894287087e-01

          -9.394476805524146767e-01,1.173889805793554952e+00,7.839521589965762122e-01
```

The columns are separated by commas, and rows are on new lines. We then close this file:

```
In [25]:  mat1file.close()
```

Now, clearly if we can save `ndarray`, we should also be able to load them. Here are some common functions for loading `ndarray`:

Load Method	Description
arr = load(file)	Loads file (either a .npy or .npz file) and stores ndarray in arr
arr = loadtxt(file, dtype, delimiter)	Loads ndarry in file, a text file, and saves to arr; optional argument delimiter gives string or character separating columns (so use delimiter=',' for a CSV file), and dtype specifies dtype (if structured, the array will be one-dimensional, with a row per datum and number of columns matching number of fields in data type)
arr = fromfile(file, count, sep)	arr is loaded from file (either an open file object or a filename), with array items separated by sep; if sep="", this will be a binary file (text otherwise); count determines number of items read (count=-1 for all)

These functions align closely to those used to save `ndarray`. You will need to save the resulting `ndarray` in Python. If you are loading from a text file, be aware that it is not necessary that the array should be created by NumPy in order for an `ndarray` to be created. This allows you to create NumPy `ndarray` in, say, a text editor or Excel if you save to a CSV. Then you can load them into Python. I presume that the data in the file you are loading is amenable to an `ndarray`; that is, it has a square format and consists of data of only one type, so no mixture of strings and numbers.

Data that is multitype can be handled by `ndarray`, but at that point you should be using a pandas DataFrame, which we will be discussing in a later section. So if I wish to load the contents of the file that I have just created, I can do so with the `loadtxt` function, and this will be the result:

```
In [26]: mat1_new = np.loadtxt("mat1.csv", delimiter=",")
         print(mat1_new)

         [[-0.03260985  1.37498789 -1.25488697]
          [-0.92670821  0.6686561  -0.13498909]
          [-0.29550081 -1.37310763  0.4636043 ]]
```

Summary

In this chapter, we started by introducing NumPy data types. We then quickly moved on to discuss NumPy arrays, called `ndarray` objects, which are the main objects of interest in NumPy. We discussed how to create these arrays from programmer input, from other Python objects, from files, and even from functions. We proceeded to discuss how mathematical operations are performed on `ndarray` objects, from basic arithmetic to full-blown linear algebra.

In the next chapter, we will discuss some important topics: slicing `ndarray` objects arithmetic and linear algebra with arrays, and employing array methods and functions.

Operations on NumPy Arrays

3

Now that we know how to create NumPy arrays, we can discuss the important topic of slicing NumPy arrays in order to access and manipulate subsets of array data. In this chapter, we will cover what every NumPy user should know about array slicing, arithmetic, linear algebra with arrays, and employing array methods and functions.

Selecting elements explicitly

If you know how to select subsets of Python lists, you know most of what you need to know about `ndarray` slicing. The elements of the array being indexed that correspond to the elements of the indexing object are returned in a new array. The most important aspect of indexing is to remember that there is more than one dimension, and the indexing method should be able to handle these other dimensions.

Remember the following points while selecting elements explicitly:

- Array slicing strongly resembles slicing lists; just remember there may be more than one dimensions

- For a one-dimensional array arr1 of length 5, we can select elements with arr1[[0, 2, 3]] (the list could be replaced with a tuple)

- A 5x3 array arr2 could be subset like arr2[[0, 2, 3]][[1, 2]], but this syntax is not preferred for ndarrays

- An equivalent and preferred subsetting would be: arr2[[0, 2, 3], [1, 2]]; the comma separates dimensions

Separate the indexing objects for different dimensions with a comma; the object before the first comma shows how the first dimension is indexed. After the first comma comes the index for the second dimension, after the second comma comes the index for the third dimension, and so on.

Slicing arrays with colons

Indexing `ndarray` objects using colons works like indexing lists using colons. Just remember there are multiple dimensions now. Remember that when the spot before or after the colon is left blank, Python treats the index as extending to either the beginning or the end of the dimension. A second colon can be specified to instruct Python to, say, skip every other row or reverse the order of rows, depending on the number under the second colon.

The following points need to be remembered when slicing arrays with colons:

- The colon works with arrays exactly like with Python lists; again, just remember there's more than one dimension
- Select all rows from a to b and all columns from c to d of the two-dimensional array arr with arr[a:b, c:d] (remember, this will not include row b or column d!)
- Select every row in a dimension with : , like arr[a:b, :]
- Select all rows up to b with arr[:b, :] (a: selects rows after and including row a)
- A second colon can be used to go by increments (say, arr[a:b:i, :]) or go in reverse direction for negative numbers (say, arr[a:b:(-1), :])

Let's see an example. First we load in NumPy and create an array:

```
In [1]:  import numpy as np

         arr1 = np.array([[["Joey", "Bob", "Sarah"],
                    Joey       ["Margaret", "Rachel", "Jim"],
                           ["Wayne", "Joey", "Liam"]],

                          [["Max", "Maxine", "Richard"],
                           ["Harold", "Curtis", "Simon"],
                           ["Bob", "Liam", "Simon"]],

                          [["Wayne", "Sarah", "Lucy"],
                           ["Lucy", "Kurtis", "Yu"],
                           ["Joey", "Lex", "Alex"]]])
         print(arr1)

         [[['Joey' 'Bob' 'Sarah']
           ['Margaret' 'Rachel' 'Jim']
           ['Wayne' 'Joey' 'Liam']]
```

Notice that what we created is a three-dimensional array. Now, this array is a bit complicated, so let's work with a two-dimensional 3 x 3 array instead:

```
In [3]: arr2 = arr1[:, :, 0].copy()
        print(arr2)

        [['Joey' 'Margaret' 'Wayne']
         ['Max' 'Harold' 'Bob']
         ['Wayne' 'Lucy' 'Joey']]
```

We used the copy method here. A new object was returned, but that object isn't a new copy of the array; it is a view of the array's contents. So if we wish to create an independent copy, we will need to use the copy method when slicing as well, as we have seen before.

If we want to change an entry in this new array, say the second row and the second column's contents to Atilla, then we change this new array:

```
In [4]: arr2[1, 1] = "Attila"
        print(arr2)

        [['Joey' 'Margaret' 'Wayne']
         ['Max' 'Attila' 'Bob']
         ['Wayne' 'Lucy' 'Joey']]
```

But we have not changed the original contents:

```
In [5]: # No attila in arr1
        print(arr1)

        [[['Joey' 'Bob' 'Sarah']
          ['Margaret' 'Rachel' 'Jim']
          ['Wayne' 'Joey' 'Liam']]

         [['Max' 'Maxine' 'Richard']
          ['Harold' 'Curtis' 'Simon']
          ['Bob' 'Liam' 'Simon']]

         [['Wayne' 'Sarah' 'Lucy']
          ['Lucy' 'Kurtis' 'Yu']
          ['Joey' 'Lex' 'Alex']]]]
```

So, these are two independent copies of the data in the first array. Now let's explore some other slicing schemes.

Here, we see indexing using lists. What we do is create a list that corresponds to the first coordinate of every element from the object we wish to capture, and then we have a list for the second coordinate. So 1 and 0 correspond to one element that we wish to select; if this were a three-dimensional object, we would need a third list for the third coordinate:

```
In [6]:  # Choose manually the "cross" elements
         print(arr2[[1, 1, 1, 0, 2], [0, 1, 2, 1, 1]])

         ['Max' 'Attila' 'Bob' 'Margaret' 'Lucy']
```

We select elements from the upper-left corner using slicers:

```
In [ ]:  # Upper-left corner
         print(arr2[:2, :2])
```

Now, let's select elements from the middle column:

```
In [8]:  # Middle column, all rows
         print(arr2[:, 1])

         ['Margaret' 'Attila' 'Lucy']
```

And, let's select elements from the middle column but we will not flatten the matrix and we'll keep its shape:

```
In [9]:  # Middle column, all rows, but don't flatten; keep matrix shape
         # When a list is used for choosing the column, the dimension is kept
         print(arr2[:, [1]])

         [['Margaret']
          ['Attila']
          ['Lucy']]
```

This is a one-dimensional object, but here we want a two-dimensional object. While it has only one column, it has one column and one row, as opposed to having only one row and columns don't make sense. Now let's select the last two rows of the middle column:

```
In [10]:  # Last two rows of middle column
          print(arr2[1:, 1])

          ['Attila' 'Lucy']
```

We reverse the row order:

```
In [11]:  # Reverse row order
          print(arr2[::-1, :])

          [['Wayne' 'Lucy' 'Joey']
           ['Max' 'Attila' 'Bob']
           ['Joey' 'Margaret' 'Wayne']]
```

If you look at the original object, you will see that these rules are happening in reverse order (compared to how they originally were ordered) and this means selecting odd number columns:

```
In [12]:  # Select odd-number columns
          print(arr2[:, 0:3:2])

          [['Joey' 'Wayne']
           ['Max' 'Bob']
           ['Wayne' 'Joey']]
```

We can go to a more complex three-dimensional array and see similar slicing schemes. For example, here's a 2 x 2 x 2 corner cube:

```
In [13]:  # Choose a 2x2x2 corner cube
          print(arr1[0:2, 0:2, 0:2])

          [[['Joey' 'Bob']
            ['Margaret' 'Rachel']]

           [['Max' 'Maxine']
            ['Harold' 'Curtis']]]
```

Here is the middle slice:

```
In [15]: print(arr1[:, 1, :].shape) # Not three-dimensional

         (3, 3)
```

We can see that this middle slice is a two-dimensional array. So, if we wish to preserve the dimensionality, another way to do so would be to use the new axis object from NumPy to insert an extra dimension:

```
In [16]: # Select middle slice, but keep an extra dimension
         print(arr1[:, 1, np.newaxis, :])

         [[['Margaret' 'Rachel' 'Jim']]

          [['Harold' 'Curtis' 'Simon']]

          [['Lucy' 'Kurtis' 'Yu']]]
```

And we see that this object is, in fact, three-dimensional:

```
In [17]: print(arr1[:, 1, np.newaxis, :].shape)

         (3, 1, 3)
```

This is in spite of the fact that the length of one of its dimensions is 1.

Advanced indexing

Let's now discuss more advanced indexing techniques. We can index ndarray objects using other ndarray. We can slice an ndarray using either ndarray objects containing integers that correspond to the indices of the ndarray we wish to select, or ndarray objects of Boolean values, where the value true means a cell should be included in the slice.

Select the elements of `arr2` that are not `Wayne`, and this is the result:

```
In [18]:   # Select all entries that are not Wayne
           print(arr2[arr2 != "Wayne"])

           ['Joey' 'Margaret' 'Max' 'Attila' 'Bob' 'Lucy' 'Joey']
```

Wayne is not included in the selection, and this was the array that was generated to do that indexing:

```
In [19]:   # A peak at the indexing boolean array
           print(arr2 != "Wayne")

           [[ True   True False]
            [ True   True  True]
            [False  True  True]]
```

It is `True` everywhere except where the contents were `Wayne`.

Another more advanced technique is to select using arrays of integers that identify which elements we want. So here, we're going to create two arrays that will be used for this slicing:

```
In [20]:   # Select, effectively, an array holding the data in the corners
           idx0 = np.array([[0, 0],
                            [2, 2]])
           idx1 = np.array([[0, 2],
                            [0, 2]])

           print(arr2[idx0, idx1])

           [['Joey' 'Wayne']
            ['Wayne' 'Joey']]
```

This first 0 in the first array means the first coordinate is zero, and the first 0 in the second array means that second coordinate is zero, as specified by the order these two arrays are listed in. So, in the first row and first column of the resulting array, we have the element [0, 0]. In the first row and second column, we have the element [0, 2] from the original array. Then, in the second row and first column, we have the element that's in the third row and first column of the original array. Notice that this was `Wayne`.

Then we have the element that was in the third row and the third column of the original array, which corresponds to `Joey`.

Let's see this with more complex arrays. For example, we can see all entries of `arr1` that are not `Curtis`:

```
In [22]:  # All entries that are not Curtis
          print(arr1[arr1 != "Curtis"])

          ['Joey' 'Bob' 'Sarah' 'Margaret' 'Rachel' 'Jim' 'Wayne' 'Joey' 'Liam' 'Max'
           'Maxine' 'Richard' 'Harold' 'Simon' 'Bob' 'Liam' 'Simon' 'Wayne' 'Sarah'
           'Lucy' 'Lucy' 'Kurtis' 'Yu' 'Joey' 'Lex' 'Alex']
```

This is what the indexing array looks like:

```
In [23]:  # A peak at the indexing array
          print(arr1 != "Curtis")

          [[[ True   True   True]
            [ True   True   True]
            [ True   True   True]]

           [[ True   True   True]
            [ True  False   True]
            [ True   True   True]]

           [[ True   True   True]
            [ True   True   True]
            [ True   True   True]]]
```

Here, we see a much more complex slicing scheme:

```
In [ ]:  # Get a 2x2x2 matrix with corner elements
         # Row indices
         idx0 = np.array([[[0, 0],
                           [0, 0]],

                          [[2, 2],
                           [2, 2]]])

         # Column indices
         idx1 = np.array([[[0, 2],
                           [0, 2]],

                          [[0, 2],
                           [0, 2]]])

         # Depth indices
         idx2 = np.array([[[0, 0],
                           [2, 2]],

                          [[0, 0],
                           [2, 2]]])

         # Notice that the (0, 0, 0) element of the sliced array will be (0, 0, 0) of arr1,
         # (1, 0, 0) of sliced array will be element (2, 0, 0) of arr1,
         # (0, 1, 0) of sliced array will be element (0, 2, 0) of arr1,
         # and so on.
         print(arr1[idx0, idx1, idx2])
```

`idx0` tells how to pick first coordinates, `idx1` tells how to pick second coordinates, and `idx2` tells how to pick third coordinates. In this case, we are selecting objects in each of the quarter elements of the original array.

So, I have actually written some code that can actually demonstrate which elements are going to show up in the new array, that is, what the coordinates from the original array are for elements of the new array.

For example, what we got was a three-dimensional matrix, 2 x 2 x 2. If we wanted to know what was in the second row, the second column, and the first slab of the sliced object, we could use code like this:

```
In [26]:  # In fact, if you want to know which element of arr1 will be in the sliced array,
          # here's some code to find out!

          coord = (1, 1, 0)  # Coord in sliced array
          print((idx0[coord], idx1[coord], idx2[coord]))

          (2, 0, 2)
```

That was element 2, 0, 2 of the original array.

Expanding arrays

The concatenate function allows binding arrays together along a common axis, using the syntax seen on the screen. This approach requires that the arrays have similar shapes along the axes not used for binding. The result is a brand new ndarray that is the product of this gluing of arrays together. Other similar functions exist for this purpose, such as stack. We will not cover all of them.

Let's suppose that we want to add more rows to arr2. Use the following code to do this:

```
# Add a new row
arr2 = np.concatenate((arr2, np.array([["Sam", "Joe", "Bill"]])), axis=0)
print(arr2)
```

We create a brand new array. We don't need to use the copy method in this situation. This is the result:

```
[['Joey' 'Margaret' 'Wayne']
 ['Max' 'Attila' 'Bob']
 ['Wayne' 'Lucy' 'Joey']
 ['Sam' 'Joe' 'Bill']]
```

We have added a fourth row to this array, binding a new array with the data (names in the array). It is still a two-dimensional array. For example, see the array in the following example. You can clearly see this is two-dimensional but has a single column, whereas the previous one has a single row, and this is the result when we add in this new column:

```
In [28]:  # Add a new column
          arr2 = np.concatenate((arr2, np.array([["Maya"], ["Nana"], ["Gus"], ["Greg"]])), axis=1)
          print(arr2)

          [['Joey' 'Margaret' 'Wayne' 'Maya']
           ['Max' 'Attila' 'Bob' 'Nana']
           ['Wayne' 'Lucy' 'Joey' 'Gus']
           ['Sam' 'Joe' 'Bill' 'Greg']]
```

We will continue with mathematical operations with arrays.

Arithmetic and linear algebra with arrays

Now that we have seen how to create and access information with NumPy arrays, let's cover some of the numerical operations you can do with arrays. In this section, we will be discussing arithmetic using NumPy arrays; we also discuss using NumPy arrays for linear algebra.

Arithmetic with two equal-shaped arrays

Arithmetic with NumPy arrays is always done component-wise. This means that, if we have two matrices that have equal shapes, an operation such as addition is done by matching corresponding components in the two matrices and adding them. This is true for any arithmetic operation, be it addition, subtraction, multiplication, division, powers, or even logical operators.

Let's see an example. First, we create two arrays of random data:

```
In [1]:  import numpy as np
         from numpy.random import randn
         import numpy.linalg as ln

         arr1 = np.array(randn(3, 3, 3) * 10, dtype = np.int64)
         arr2 = np.array(randn(3, 3, 3) * 10, dtype = np.int64)
         print(arr1)

         [[[ 11 -13  -5]
           [  0 -16   4]
           [ 12   0   6]]

          [[ -8   6   0]
           [  4  -9   4]
           [  1  -6   8]]

          [[  5   3   3]
           [  6 -22  -2]
           [ 10   1  -4]]]]
```

```
In [2]:  print(arr2)

         [[[  8   8  10]
          [ -4   0  -7]
          [-12  -8 -19]]

          [[ 28   3  -8]
          [ -2   9   9]
          [  9  -9  -6]]

          [[  2   3  -4]
          [ -2  -4   7]
          [ 12  -6   5]]]]
```

While I explain these ideas in terms of arithmetic involving two arrays, it can involve arrays and scalars as we see here, where we add 100 to every element in arr1:

```
In [3]:  print(arr1 + 100)

         [[[111  87  95]
          [100  84 104]
          [112 100 106]]

          [[ 92 106 100]
          [104  91 104]
          [101  94 108]]

          [[105 103 103]
          [106  78  98]
          [110 101  96]]]]
```

Next, we divide every element in `arr1` by 2:

```
In [4]: print(arr1 / 2)

        [[[  5.5  -6.5  -2.5]
         [  0.   -8.    2. ]
         [  6.    0.    3. ]]

        [[ -4.    3.    0. ]
         [  2.   -4.5   2. ]
         [  0.5  -3.    4. ]]

        [[  2.5   1.5   1.5]
         [  3.  -11.   -1. ]
         [  5.    0.5  -2. ]]]
```

Next, we raise every element in `arr1` to the power of 2:

```
In [5]: print(arr1 ** 2)

        [[[121 169  25]
         [  0 256  16]
         [144   0  36]]

        [[ 64  36   0]
         [ 16  81  16]
         [  1  36  64]]

        [[ 25   9   9]
         [ 36 484   4]
         [100   1  16]]]
```

And next, we multiply the contents of `arr1` and `arr2`:

```
In [6]:  print(arr1 * arr2)
         [[[  88 -104  -50]
          [   0    0  -28]
          [-144    0 -114]]

         [[-224   18    0]
          [  -8  -81   36]
          [   9   54  -48]]

         [[  10    9  -12]
          [ -12   88  -14]
          [ 120   -6  -20]]]
```

Notice that both `arr1` and `arr2` have similar shapes. Here, we do an even more complex computation involving these two arrays:

```
In [7]:  print(arr1 ** (arr2 / 4))    # Watch out for nan and inf!
         [[[  1.21000000e+02   1.69000000e+02               nan]
          [              inf   1.00000000e+00   8.83883476e-02]
          [  5.78703704e-04               inf   2.01271165e-04]]

         [[ -2.09715200e+06   3.83365863e+00               inf]
          [  5.00000000e-01               nan   2.26274170e+01]
          [  1.00000000e+00               nan   4.41941738e-02]]

         [[  2.23606798e+00   2.27950706e+00   3.33333333e-01]
          [  4.08248290e-01  -4.54545455e-02               nan]
          [  1.00000000e+03   1.00000000e+00               nan]]]
C:\Anaconda3\lib\site-packages\ipykernel\__main__.py:1: RuntimeWarning: divide by zero encountered in power
```

Notice that this computation ended up producing `inf` and `nan`.

Broadcasting

So far, we have worked with two arrays with equal shape. In fact, this is not necessary. While we cannot necessarily add two arrays of any shape, there are situations where we can reasonably perform an arithmetic operation on arrays of different shapes. In some sense, information in a smaller array is treated as if it belongs to an array of equal shapes, but with repeated values. Let's see some of this broadcasting behavior in action.

Now, recall that the array `arr1` is 3 x 3 x 3; that is, it has three rows, three columns, and three slabs. Here, we create an object, `arr3`:

```
In [9]:  print(arr3.shape)

         (1, 1, 3)
```

This object has the shape `(1, 1, 3)`. So, this object has the same number of slabs as `arr1`, but it has only one row and one column. This is a situation where broadcasting can be applied; in fact, this is the result:

```
In [10]:  print(arr1 * arr3)

          [[[  0 -13   0]
           [  0 -16   0]
           [  0   0   0]]

          [[  0   6   0]
           [  0  -9   0]
           [  0  -6   0]]

          [[  0   3   0]
           [  0 -22   0]
           [  0   1   0]]]
```

I had column 0 and column 2 as 0, and the middle column as 1. So the result is that I am effectively selecting the middle column and making the other two columns 0. This object was effectively replicated so that it looked as if I was multiplying `arr1` by an object, where there are 0s in the first column, 0s in the third column, and 1s in the second column.

Now, let's see what happens if we switch up the dimensions of this object; so now it has one column, one slab, and three rows:

```
In [11]:  arr4 = arr3.transpose((0, 2, 1))
          print(arr4)

          [[[0]
            [1]
            [0]]]
```

And this is the result:

```
In [12]:  print(arr1 * arr4)

          [[[  0   0   0]
            [  0 -16   4]
            [  0   0   0]]

           [[  0   0   0]
            [  4  -9   4]
            [  0   0   0]]

           [[  0   0   0]
            [  6 -22  -2]
            [  0   0   0]]]]
```

Now, let's do another transposition. We're going to end up multiplying an object that has three slabs, and the middle slab is filled with 1s. So when I do the multiplication, this is what happens:

```
In [13]:  arr5 = arr3.transpose((2, 0, 1))
          print(arr5)

          [[[0]]

           [[1]]

           [[0]]]

In [14]:  print(arr1 * arr5)

          [[[  0   0   0]
            [  0   0   0]
            [  0   0   0]]

           [[ -8   6   0]
            [  4  -9   4]
            [  1  -6   8]]]
```

Linear algebra

Be aware that NumPy is built to support linear algebra. A 1D NumPy array may correspond to a linear algebra vector; a 2D array to a matrix; and 3D, 4D, or all `ndarray` to tensors. So, when appropriate, NumPy supports linear algebra operations, such as matrix products, transposition, matrix inversion, and so on, for arrays. Most NumPy linear algebra functionality is supported in the `linalg` module. The following is a list of commonly used NumPy linear algebra functions:

Method	Name	Description
arr1.transpose(shape) arr1.T	Transposition	Rows become columns, columns become rows by default (and always for T); if a tuple is supplied, swaps axes as instructed by the tuple
arr1.reshape(newshape)	Reshape	Given a tuple, "unravels" an array and creates an array with the new shape
dot(a, b)	Matrix product	Computes the matrix product of two 2D arrays
matrix_power(m, n)	Matrix power	Raises square 2D array m to power n, thinking of power in the sense of matrix products
inv(a)	Matrix inverse	Finds a square 2D array's inverse
trace(a)	Trace	Sum of diagonal elements
det(a)	Determinant	Computer the determinant of a 2D array
eig(a)	Eigenvalues and eigenvectors	Get the eigenvalues and right eigenvectors of a 2D array
svd(a)	Singular value decomposition	Finds the singular-value decomposition of an array

Some of these are `ndarray` methods, others are in the `linalg` module you need to import. So we've actually been demonstrating transpose up to this point in earlier examples. Notice that we were using transpose here to swap around rows and columns.

This is transposition in `arr4`:

```
In [11]: arr4 = arr3.transpose((0, 2, 1))
         print(arr4)

         [[[0]
           [1]
           [0]]]
```

I said `arr4` was `arr3` and we switched around the axes. So axis 0 would still be axis 0, but axis 1 would be axis 2 of the old array, and axis 2 would be axis 1 of the old array.

Now let's see some other examples. Let's see a demonstration of reshape. So the first thing we do is create an array consisting of eight elements:

```
In [16]: arr6 = np.arange(0, 8)
         print(arr6)

         [0 1 2 3 4 5 6 7]
```

We can rearrange the contents of this array so that it fits into an array of a different shape. Now, what is required is that the new array has the same number of elements as the original array. So, create a 2 x 4 array as follows:

```
In [17]: print(arr6.reshape(2, 4))     # Notice 2 * 4 = 8

         [[0 1 2 3]
          [4 5 6 7]]
```

It has eight elements, just as the original array did. Also, it created an array where the first row consists of the first four elements of the original array, and the second row contains the remaining elements. I could do a similar manipulation with `arr6`:

```
In [18]: print(arr6.reshape(2, 2, 2))    # 2 * 2 * 2 = 8

         [[[0 1]
           [2 3]]

          [[4 5]
           [6 7]]]
```

You can kind of guess by looking at this array how the logic was done.

Now let's see some more complex linear algebra functionality. Let's load in, from the datasets module of the Scikit-Learn library, a function called `load_iris`, so that we can look at the classic Iris dataset:

```
In [19]: from sklearn.datasets import load_iris
         # Load iris data set
         iris = load_iris().data[:, :]
         print(iris)
         [ 4.8  3.   1.4  0.1]
         [ 4.3  3.   1.1  0.1]
         [ 5.8  4.   1.2  0.2]
         [ 5.7  4.4  1.5  0.4]
         [ 5.4  3.9  1.3  0.4]
         [ 5.1  3.5  1.4  0.3]
         [ 5.7  3.8  1.7  0.3]
         [ 5.1  3.8  1.5  0.3]
         [ 5.4  3.4  1.7  0.2]
         [ 5.1  3.7  1.5  0.4]
         [ 4.6  3.6  1.   0.2]
         [ 5.1  3.3  1.7  0.5]
         [ 4.8  3.4  1.9  0.2]
         [ 5.   3.   1.6  0.2]
         [ 5.   3.4  1.6  0.4]
         [ 5.2  3.5  1.5  0.2]
         [ 5.2  3.4  1.4  0.2]
         [ 4.7  3.2  1.6  0.2]
         [ 4.8  3.1  1.6  0.2]
         [ 5.4  3.4  1.5  0.4]
```

So the following is a transpose of `iris`:

```
In [20]: print(iris.T)

[[ 5.1  4.9  4.7  4.6  5.   5.4  4.6  5.   4.4  4.9  5.4  4.8  4.8  4.3
   5.8  5.7  5.4  5.1  5.7  5.1  5.4  5.1  4.6  5.1  4.8  5.   5.   5.2
   5.2  4.7  4.8  5.4  5.2  5.5  4.9  5.   5.5  4.9  4.4  5.1  5.   4.5
   4.4  5.   5.1  4.8  5.1  4.6  5.3  5.   7.   6.4  6.9  5.5  6.5  5.7
   6.3  4.9  6.6  5.2  5.   5.9  6.   6.1  5.6  6.7  5.6  5.8  6.2  5.6
   5.9  6.1  6.3  6.1  6.4  6.6  6.8  6.7  6.   5.7  5.5  5.5  5.8  6.   5.4
   6.   6.7  6.3  5.6  5.5  5.5  6.1  5.8  5.   5.6  5.7  5.7  6.2  5.1
   5.7  6.3  5.8  7.1  6.3  6.5  7.6  4.9  7.3  6.7  7.2  6.5  6.4  6.8
   5.7  5.8  6.4  6.5  7.7  7.7  6.   6.9  5.6  7.7  6.3  6.7  7.2  6.2
   6.1  6.4  7.2  7.4  7.9  6.4  6.3  6.1  7.7  6.3  6.4  6.   6.9  6.7
   6.9  5.8  6.8  6.7  6.7  6.3  6.5  6.2  5.9]
 [ 3.5  3.   3.2  3.1  3.6  3.9  3.4  3.4  2.9  3.1  3.7  3.4  3.   3.   4.
   4.4  3.9  3.5  3.8  3.8  3.4  3.7  3.6  3.3  3.4  3.   3.4  3.5  3.4
   3.2  3.1  3.4  4.1  4.2  3.1  3.2  3.5  3.1  3.   3.4  3.5  2.3  3.2
   3.5  3.8  3.   3.8  3.2  3.7  3.3  3.2  3.2  3.1  2.3  2.8  2.8  3.3
   2.4  2.9  2.7  2.   3.   2.2  2.9  2.9  3.1  3.   2.7  2.2  2.5  3.2
   2.8  2.5  2.8  2.9  3.   2.8  3.   2.9  2.6  2.4  2.4  2.7  2.7  3.   3.4
   3.1  2.3  3.   2.5  2.6  3.   2.6  2.3  2.7  3.   2.9  2.9  2.5  2.8
   3.3  2.7  3.   2.9  3.   3.   2.5  2.9  2.5  3.6  3.2  2.7  3.   2.5
   2.8  3.2  3.   3.8  2.6  2.2  3.2  2.8  2.8  2.7  3.3  3.2  2.8  3.   2.8
   3.   2.8  3.8  2.8  2.8  2.6  3.   3.4  3.1  3.   3.1  3.1  3.1  2.7
   3.2  3.3  3.   2.5  3.   3.4  3. ]
 [ 1.4  1.4  1.3  1.5  1.4  1.7  1.4  1.5  1.4  1.5  1.5  1.6  1.4  1.1
   1.2  1.5  1.3  1.4  1.7  1.5  1.7  1.5  1.   1.7  1.9  1.6  1.6  1.5
   1.4  1.6  1.6  1.5  1.5  1.4  1.5  1.2  1.3  1.5  1.3  1.5  1.3  1.3
   1.3  1.6  1.9  1.4  1.6  1.4  1.5  1.4  4.7  4.5  4.9  4.   4.6  4.5
   4.7  3.3  4.6  3.9  3.5  4.2  4.   4.7  3.6  4.4  4.5  4.1  4.5  3.9
   4.8  4.   4.9  4.7  4.3  4.4  4.8  5.   4.5  3.5  3.8  3.7  3.9  5.1
   4.5  4.5  4.7  4.4  4.1  4.   4.4  4.6  4.   3.3  4.2  4.2  4.2  4.3  3.
   4.1  6.   5.1  5.9  5.6  5.8  6.6  4.5  6.3  5.8  6.1  5.1  5.3  5.5  5.
```

Make a copy of this array, as follows:

```
In [21]:  iris_cp = iris.copy()
          iris_cp

Out[21]:  array([[ 5.1,  3.5,  1.4,  0.2],
                 [ 4.9,  3. ,  1.4,  0.2],
                 [ 4.7,  3.2,  1.3,  0.2],
                 [ 4.6,  3.1,  1.5,  0.2],
                 [ 5. ,  3.6,  1.4,  0.2],
                 [ 5.4,  3.9,  1.7,  0.4],
                 [ 4.6,  3.4,  1.4,  0.3],
                 [ 5. ,  3.4,  1.5,  0.2],
                 [ 4.4,  2.9,  1.4,  0.2],
                 [ 4.9,  3.1,  1.5,  0.1],
                 [ 5.4,  3.7,  1.5,  0.2],
                 [ 4.8,  3.4,  1.6,  0.2],
                 [ 4.8,  3. ,  1.4,  0.1],
                 [ 4.3,  3. ,  1.1,  0.1],
                 [ 5.8,  4. ,  1.2,  0.2],
                 [ 5.7,  4.4,  1.5,  0.4],
                 [ 5.4,  3.9,  1.3,  0.4],
                 [ 5.1,  3.5,  1.4,  0.3],
                 [ 5.7,  3.8,  1.7,  0.3],
                 [ 5.1,  3.8,  1.5,  0.3],
```

I also want to create a new array that consists of only the last column of the copy of Iris, and I create another array consisting of the remaining columns and also a column of 1s.

Now, we're going to create a new array that will correspond to a matrix product. So I say X squared is X transposed and multiplied by X, and this is the resulting array:

```
In [24]:  # Matrix product
          X_sq = X.T.dot(X)
          print(X_sq)

          [[  150.      876.5     458.1     563.8 ]
           [  876.5    5223.85   2670.98   3484.25]
           [  458.1    2670.98   1427.05   1673.91]
           [  563.8    3484.25   1673.91   2583.  ]]
```

It is 4 x 4. Now let's get an inverse, the matrix X squared.

This is going to be the matrix inverse:

```
In [25]: # Matrix inverse
         X_sq_inv = ln.inv(X_sq)
         print(X_sq_inv)

         [[ 0.86171781 -0.13800334 -0.06693333  0.04144097]
          [-0.13800334  0.06129955 -0.03658066 -0.02885944]
          [-0.06693333 -0.03658066  0.06519657  0.02170344]
          [ 0.04144097 -0.02885944  0.02170344  0.01620576]]
```

I then take this inverse and then multiply it with the product of the transpose of X with the matrix Y, which is that one-column matrix that I created earlier. And this is the result:

```
In [26]: beta = X_sq_inv.dot(X.T.dot(y))
         print(beta)     # Coefficients of a linear model

         [-0.24872359 -0.21027133  0.22877721  0.52608818]
```

This is not some arbitrary sequence of computations; it actually corresponds to how we solve for coefficients of a linear model. The original matrix, `y = iris_cp[:, 3]`, corresponds to the value of a variable that we want to predict, using the contents of X; but for now I just want to demonstrate some of the linear algebra. Whenever you encounter a function that fits a linear model, you now know all the code that you need to write this function yourself.

Another thing that we often do in data analysis is find the SVD decomposition of a matrix, and the SVD decomposition is provided in this linear algebra function:

```
In [27]: # SVD decomposition of iris_cp
         iris_svd = ln.svd(iris_cp)
         print(iris_svd[1])     # Spectral values of iris_cp

         [ 95.95066751  17.7229532    3.46929666   1.87891236]
```

So the last line corresponds to the spectral values. **Spectral value decomposition (SVD)** and the values in the output are the spectral values of a matrix. The following are the left singular vectors:

```
In [28]:  # Left-singular vectors
          print(iris_svd[0])

          [[ -6.16171172e-02   1.29969428e-01  -5.58364155e-05 ...,  -9.34637342e-02
             -9.60224157e-02  -8.09922905e-02]
           [ -5.80722977e-02   1.11371452e-01   6.84386629e-02 ...,   3.66755322e-02
             -3.24463474e-02   1.27273399e-02]
           [ -5.67633852e-02   1.18294769e-01   2.31062793e-03 ...,   3.08252776e-02
              1.95234663e-01   1.35567696e-01]

           ...,
           [ -9.40702260e-02  -4.98348018e-02  -4.14958083e-02 ...,   9.81822841e-01
             -2.17978813e-02  -8.85972146e-03]
           [ -9.48993908e-02  -5.62107520e-02  -2.12386574e-01 ...,  -2.14264126e-02
              9.42038920e-01  -2.96933496e-02]
           [ -8.84882764e-02  -5.16210172e-02  -9.51442925e-02 ...,  -8.52768485e-03
             -3.02139863e-02   9.73577349e-01]]
```

These are the right singular vectors:

```
In [29]:  print(iris_svd[0].shape)

          (150, 150)


In [30]:  # Right-signular vectors
          print(iris_svd[2])

          [[-0.75116805 -0.37978837 -0.51315094 -0.16787934]
           [ 0.28583096  0.54488976 -0.70889874 -0.34475845]
           [ 0.49942378 -0.67502499 -0.05471983 -0.54029889]
           [ 0.32345496 -0.32124324 -0.48077482  0.74902286]]


In [31]:  print(iris_svd[2].shape)

          (4, 4)
```

Employing array methods and functions

We will now discuss the use of NumPy array methods and functions. In this section, we will look at common `ndarray` functions and methods. These features allow you to perform common tasks using a clean, intuitive syntax, going beyond the notion of Pythonic code.

Array methods

NumPy `ndarray` functions include methods that facilitate common tasks, such as finding the mean of a dataset or multiple means of multiple datasets. We can sort array rows and columns, find mathematical and statistical measures, and much more. There are so many functions that do so many things! I won't list them all. In the following, we see the functions needed for common administrative tasks, such as interpreting arrays as lists or sorting array contents:

Method	Description
arr1.tolist()	Converts an ndarray to a Python list
arr1.view()	Create a new view of an ndarray
arr1.flatten()	Flatten an ndarray to a 1D array
arr1.squeeze()	Remove length-one dimensions
arr1.repeat(repeats)	Repeat array elements of arr1, as specified by repeats
arr1.sort(axis) arr1.argsort(axis)	Sorts arr1 in-place along dimension specified by axis; argsort() returns, instead, the order of the indices of the original array if it were sorted
arr1.fill(a)	Fill arr1 with a

Next, we see common statistical and mathematical methods, such as finding the mean or sum of array contents:

Method	Description
arr1.min(axis) arr1.max(axis)	Creates an array containing the minimum/maximum along dimensions specified by axis
arr1.argmin(axis) arr1.argmax(axis)	Like min/max but instead of returning the min/max, returns the index corresponding to the min/max
arr1.sum(axis) arr1.mean(axis) arr1.std(axis) arr1.var(axis)	Creates an array containing the sum/mean/standard deviation/variance of data along the dimension specified by axis
arr1.cumsum(axis)	Returns an array consisting of the cumulative sum of elements along the dimension specified by axis
arr1.round(decimals)	Rounds the elements in arr1 to number of decimal spaces specified by decimals

We also have methods for arrays of Boolean values:

Method	Description
arr1.any(axis)	If axis is not specified, returns True if any element of arr1 is True; if axis is specified, does the same, but along dimension specified by axis
arr1.all(axis)	Like any(), but returns True only if all elements are True

Let's see some of these in a Notebook. Import NumPy and create an array of random values:

```
In [1]:  import numpy as np
         from numpy.random import randn

         arr1 = np.array(randn(4, 4) * 10, dtype = np.int8)
         print(arr1)

         [[  8    3  12   -2]
          [  4  -15    3    3]
          [-10   -3    2   -5]
          [  0   -5  -26   -3]]
```

Let's see some of the manipulations we can do on this array. One thing we can do is coerce the array into a list:

```
In [2]:  arr1.tolist()      # Turn arr1 to a List
Out[2]:  [[8, 3, 12, -2], [4, -15, 3, 3], [-10, -3, 2, -5], [0, -5, -26, -3]]
```

We can flatten the array so that it goes from being a 4 x 4 array to a 1D array, as follows:

```
In [3]:  arr1.flatten()     # Make a 1D array
Out[3]:  array([  8,   3,  12,  -2,   4, -15,   3,   3, -10,  -3,   2,  -5,   0,
                 -5, -26,  -3], dtype=int8)
```

We can also fill an empty array with the fill method. Here, I create an empty array that is intended for strings, and I fill it with the string `Carlos`:

```
In [4]:  arr2 = np.empty((4, 3), dtype=np.dtype('<U16'))    # An empty array for strings
         arr2.fill("Carlos")   # Fill with "Carlos", in-place (make changes to the array, not a new one)
         arr2

Out[4]:  array([['Carlos', 'Carlos', 'Carlos'],
                ['Carlos', 'Carlos', 'Carlos'],
                ['Carlos', 'Carlos', 'Carlos'],
                ['Carlos', 'Carlos', 'Carlos']],
               dtype='<U16')
```

We can take the contents of an array and sum them all together:

```
In [5]:  arr1.sum()

Out[5]:  -34
```

They can also sum along axes. Next, we sum along rows:

```
In [6]:  arr1.sum(axis=0)

Out[6]:  array([  2, -20,  -9,  -7])
```

And in the following, we sum along columns:

```
In [7]:  arr1.sum(axis=1)

Out[7]:  array([ 21,  -5, -16, -34])
```

Cumulative sums allow you to perform the following, instead of summing the entire contents of, say, the rows:

- Sum the first row
- Then sum the first and second rows
- Then the first, second, and third rows
- Then the first second, third, and fourth rows, and so on

This can be seen next:

```
In [8]:  arr1.cumsum(axis=0)
Out[8]:  array([[  8,    3,   12,   -2],
                [ 12,  -12,   15,    1],
                [  2,  -15,   17,   -4],
                [  2,  -20,   -9,   -7]], dtype=int32)
```

Vectorization with ufuncs

ufuncs are special NumPy functions designed to work with arrays; in particular, they support vectorization. A vectorized function is applied component-wise to the elements of an array. These are often highly optimized functions, running under the hood on a faster language, such as C.

In the following, we see some common ufuncs, many of which are mathematical:

Method	Description
sqrt(a)	Square roots
abs(a)	Absolute values
exp(a)	Computes e^x
sign(a)	The sign (+ or -) of a
sin(a) cos(a) tan(a)	Trigonometric functions
isnan(a)	Identify nan
isinf(a) isfinite(a)	Identify infinite/finite values

Let's explore some applications of ufuncs. The first thing we're going to do is find the sign of every element in arr1, that is, whether it is positive, negative, or zero:

```
In [10]: np.sign(arr1)

Out[10]: array([[ 1,  1,  1, -1],
                [ 1, -1,  1,  1],
                [-1, -1,  1, -1],
                [ 0, -1, -1, -1]], dtype=int8)
```

Then with this sign, I multiply this array with arr1. The result is as if we took the absolute value of arr1:

```
In [11]: arr1 * np.sign(arr1)     # ALL entries are positive now

Out[11]: array([[ 8,  3, 12,  2],
                [ 4, 15,  3,  3],
                [10,  3,  2,  5],
                [ 0,  5, 26,  3]], dtype=int8)
```

Now, we find the square root of the contents of the product. Since every element is non-negative, the square root is well-defined:

```
In [12]: np.sqrt(arr1 * np.sign(arr1))

Out[12]: array([[ 2.82842708, 1.73205078, 3.46410155, 1.41421354],
                [ 2.        , 3.87298346, 1.73205078, 1.73205078],
                [ 3.1622777 , 1.73205078, 1.41421354, 2.23606801],
                [ 0.        , 2.23606801, 5.09901953, 1.73205078]], dtype=float32)
```

Custom ufuncs

As mentioned earlier, we can create our own ufuncs. One way to create ufuncs is to use existing ufuncs, vectorized operations, array methods, and so on (that is, all of Numpy's existing infrastructure) to create a function that, component-wise, produces the results we want. Let's say that we didn't want to do this for some reason. If we have an existing Python function, and we merely want to make that function vectorized so that it applies to an ndarray component-wise, we can create a new vectorized version of the function with NumPy's vectorize function. Vectorize takes a function as input and gives a vectorized version of the function as output.

Vectorize is okay to use if you don't care about speed, but the function created with vectorize is not necessarily fast. In fact, the former approach (using NumPy's existing functions and infrastructure to create your vectorized function) produces ufuncs many times faster.

The first thing we're going to do is define a function that works for a single scalar value. What it does is truncate, so if a number is below zero, that number is replaced with zero:

```
In [13]: def tr(a):
             if (a > 0):
                 return a
             else:
                 return 0

         # Testing tr()
         tr(20)

Out[13]: 20

In [14]: tr(-20)
```

This function is not vectorized; let's attempt to apply this function to our matrix arr1:

```
In [15]: # Every False should be 0, according to tr(a)
         print(arr1 > 0)

         [[ True  True   True False]
          [ True False  True   True]
          [False False  True False]
          [False False False False]]
```

Then, what we would hope is that every quantity that is false in this matrix is zero instead. But when we attempt to apply this function, it simply doesn't work:

```
In [16]: tr(arr1)    # Won't work
---------------------------------------------------------------------------
ValueError                                Traceback (most recent call last)
<ipython-input-16-0c7a4f0c2236> in <module>()
----> 1 tr(arr1)      # Won't work

<ipython-input-13-bb3c045db890> in tr(a)
      1 def tr(a):
----> 2     if (a > 0):
      3         return a
      4     else:
      5         return 0

ValueError: The truth value of an array with more than one element is ambiguous. Use a.any() or a.all()
```

What we need to do is create a `ufunc` that does the same job as the original function. So we use vectorize and can create a vectorized version that works as expected, but it is not very efficient:

```
In [17]: tr_vec = np.vectorize(tr)    # vectorize() takes a function as an argument and returns a function
         tr_vec(arr1)
Out[17]: array([[ 8,  3, 12,  0],
                [ 4,  0,  3,  3],
                [ 0,  0,  2,  0],
                [ 0,  0,  0,  0]], dtype=int8)
```

We can see this by creating a much faster version that uses NumPy's existing infrastructure, such as indexing based on Boolean values, and assigning values to zero. Here is the resulting `ufunc`:

```
In [18]: def tr_vec_fast(arr):
             ret_arr = arr.copy()
             ret_arr[arr <= 0] = 0
             return ret_arr

         tr_vec_fast(arr1)
Out[18]: array([[ 8,  3, 12,  0],
                [ 4,  0,  3,  3],
                [ 0,  0,  2,  0],
                [ 0,  0,  0,  0]], dtype=int8)
```

Let's compare the speed of these two functions. The following is the vectorized version created with vectorize:

```
In [19]:  %timeit tr_vec(arr1)

          1000 loops, best of 3: 210 µs per loop
```

Next is the one that is created manually:

```
In [20]:  %timeit tr_vec_fast(arr1)
          The slowest run took 4.59 times longer than the fastest. This could mean that an intermediate result is being cached.
          10000 loops, best of 3: 27.5 µs per loop
```

Notice that the first function was much slower than the second one, which was created manually. In fact, it was almost 10 times slower.

Summary

In this chapter, we started off by selecting elements in an array explicitly. We looked into advanced indexing, and expanding arrays. We also covered some arithmetic and linear algebra with arrays. We discussed employing array methods and functions and vectorization with ufuncs. In the next chapter, we will begin learning about another influential package called **pandas**.

4

pandas are Fun! What is pandas?

We've talked about NumPy in previous chapters. Now let's move on to pandas, a well-designed package for storing, managing, and manipulating data in Python. We'll start this chapter by discussing what pandas is and why people use it. Next, we'll discuss the two most important objects provided by pandas: series and DataFrames. We will then cover how to subset your data. In this chapter, we'll get a brief overview of what pandas is, and why it's popular.

What does pandas do?

pandas introduces two key objects to Python, series and DataFrames, with the latter arguably being the most useful, but pandas DataFrames can be thought of as series bound together. A series is a sequence of data, like a list in basic Python or a 1D NumPy array. And, like the NumPy array, a series has a single data type, but indexing with a series is different. With NumPy there is not much control over row and column indices; but with a series, each element in the series must have a unique index, name, key, however you want to think about it. The index could consist of strings, such as cities in a nation, with the corresponding elements of the series denoting some statistical value, such as the city's population; or dates, such as trading days for a stock series.

A DataFrame can be thought of as multiple series of common length, with a common index, bound together in a single tabular object. This object resembles a NumPy 2D `ndarray`, but it is not the same thing. Not all columns need to be of the same data type. Going back to the cities example, we could have a column containing population and another containing the state or province in which the city is located, and yet another column containing Boolean values to identify whether the city is a state or province capital—a tricky feat to pull off with just NumPy. Each of these columns likely has a unique name, a string to identify the information they contain; perhaps this can be thought of as a variable. With this object, we can store, access, and manipulate our data easily and efficiently.

In the following Notebook, we're going to see a preview of what we can do with series and DataFrames:

```
In [1]:   import numpy as np
          import pandas as pd
```

We're going to load in both NumPy and pandas, and we are going to look at reading a CSV file in both NumPy and pandas. We can, in fact, load CSV files in NumPy, and they can have different types of data, but in order to manage such files, you need to create a custom `dtype` to resemble such data. So here we have a CSV file, `iris.csv`, which contains the Iris dataset.

Now, if we wish to load this in, we need to account for the fact that every row has data that isn't necessarily of the same type. In particular, the last column is for species, and this is not numeric but instead a string. So we need to create a custom `dtype`, which we do here, calling this new `dtype` schema:

```
In [2]:  schema = np.dtype([('sepal_length', np.float16),     # Need to define a custom dtype to read CSV of mixed data type
                            ('sepal_width',  np.float16),
                            ('petal_length', np.float16),
                            ('petal_width',  np.float16),
                            ('species',      '<U16')])
```

We can load in this dataset with the NumPy function `loadtxt`, giving the `dtype` as the `schema` object, and setting the delimiter to comma to indicate it is a CSV file. We can, in fact, read this dataset in:

```
In [4]:  np_data = np.loadtxt("iris.csv", skiprows=1, dtype=schema, delimiter=',')
```

Note that this dataset must be in your working directory. If we were to look at this dataset, this is what we would notice:

```
In [5]: np_data

Out[5]: array([( 5.1015625 , 3.5       , 1.40039062, 0.19995117, 'setosa'),
               ( 4.8984375 , 3.        , 1.40039062, 0.19995117, 'setosa'),
               ( 4.69921875, 3.19921875, 1.29980469, 0.19995117, 'setosa'),
               ( 4.6015625 , 3.09960938, 1.5       , 0.19995117, 'setosa'),
               ( 5.        , 3.59960938, 1.40039062, 0.19995117, 'setosa'),
               ( 5.3984375 , 3.90039062, 1.70019531, 0.39990234, 'setosa'),
               ( 4.6015625 , 3.40039062, 1.40039062, 0.30004883, 'setosa'),
               ( 5.        , 3.40039062, 1.5       , 0.19995117, 'setosa'),
               ( 4.3984375 , 2.90039062, 1.40039062, 0.19995117, 'setosa'),
               ( 4.8984375 , 3.09960938, 1.5       , 0.09997559, 'setosa'),
               ( 5.3984375 , 3.69921875, 1.5       , 0.19995117, 'setosa'),
               ( 4.80078125, 3.40039062, 1.59960938, 0.19995117, 'setosa'),
               ( 4.80078125, 3.        , 1.40039062, 0.09997559, 'setosa'),
               ( 4.30078125, 3.        , 1.09960938, 0.09997559, 'setosa'),
               ( 5.80078125, 4.        , 1.20019531, 0.19995117, 'setosa'),
               ( 5.69921875, 4.3984375 , 1.5       , 0.39990234, 'setosa'),
               ( 5.3984375 , 3.90039062, 1.29980469, 0.39990234, 'setosa'),
               ( 5.1015625 , 3.5       , 1.40039062, 0.30004883, 'setosa'),
               ( 5.69921875, 3.80078125, 1.70019531, 0.30004883, 'setosa'),
               ( 5.1015625 , 3.80078125, 1.5       , 0.30004883, 'setosa'),
               ( 5.3984375 , 3.40039062, 1.70019531, 0.19995117, 'setosa'),
               ( 5.1015625 , 3.69921875, 1.5       , 0.39990234, 'setosa'),
               ( 4.6015625 , 3.59960938, 1.        , 0.19995117, 'setosa'),
               ( 5.1015625 , 3.30078125, 1.70019531, 0.5       , 'setosa'),
```

This output screenshot is just for representation, and the actual output contains more lines. Every row of this dataset is a new entry in this one-dimensional NumPy array. This is, in fact, a NumPy array:

```
In [6]: type(np_data)
Out[6]: numpy.ndarray
```

We select the first five rows with the following command:

```
In [7]: np_data[:5]   # Slicing operations
Out[7]: array([( 5.1015625 , 3.5       , 1.40039062, 0.19995117, 'setosa'),
               ( 4.8984375 , 3.        , 1.40039062, 0.19995117, 'setosa'),
               ( 4.69921875, 3.19921875, 1.29980469, 0.19995117, 'setosa'),
               ( 4.6015625 , 3.09960938, 1.5       , 0.19995117, 'setosa'),
               ( 5.        , 3.59960938, 1.40039062, 0.19995117, 'setosa')],
               dtype=[('sepal_length', '<f2'), ('sepal_width', '<f2'), ('petal_length', '<f2'), ('petal_width', '<f2'), ('species', '<U16')])
```

We can select the first five rows and specify that we want to work with just sepal lengths, which are the first elements in each row:

```
In [8]: np_data[:5]['sepal_length']
Out[8]: array([ 5.1015625 ,  4.8984375 ,  4.69921875, 4.6015625 ,  5.        ], dtype=float16)
```

And we can even select petal length and species:

```
In [9]: np_data[:5][['petal_length', 'species']]
Out[9]: array([( 1.40039062, 'setosa'), ( 1.40039062, 'setosa'),
               ( 1.29980469, 'setosa'), ( 1.5       , 'setosa'),
               ( 1.40039062, 'setosa')],
              dtype=[('petal_length', '<f2'), ('species', '<U16')])
```

But there is a better way to do this with pandas. In pandas, what we will do is use the `read_csv` function, which will automatically parse the CSV file correctly:

```
In [10]: pd_data = pd.read_csv("iris.csv")

In [11]: pd_data
Out[11]:
```

	sepal_length	sepal_width	petal_length	petal_width	species
0	5.1	3.5	1.4	0.2	setosa
1	4.9	3.0	1.4	0.2	setosa
2	4.7	3.2	1.3	0.2	setosa
3	4.6	3.1	1.5	0.2	setosa
4	5.0	3.6	1.4	0.2	setosa
5	5.4	3.9	1.7	0.4	setosa
6	4.6	3.4	1.4	0.3	setosa
7	5.0	3.4	1.5	0.2	setosa
8	4.4	2.9	1.4	0.2	setosa
9	4.9	3.1	1.5	0.1	setosa
10	5.4	3.7	1.5	0.2	setosa

Look at this dataset and notice that, with Jupyter notebooks, it's presented much more readably. This is, in fact, a `pandas` DataFrame:

```
In [12]:  type(pd_data)

Out[12]:  pandas.core.frame.DataFrame
```

The first five rows can be seen using the `head` function:

```
In [13]:  pd_data.head()

Out[13]:
```

	sepal_length	sepal_width	petal_length	petal_width	species
0	5.1	3.5	1.4	0.2	setosa
1	4.9	3.0	1.4	0.2	setosa
2	4.7	3.2	1.3	0.2	setosa
3	4.6	3.1	1.5	0.2	setosa
4	5.0	3.6	1.4	0.2	setosa

We can also see the sepal length, by specifying it as if it were an attribute of this DataFrame:

```
In [14]:  pd_data.head().sepal_length

Out[14]:  0    5.1
          1    4.9
          2    4.7
          3    4.6
          4    5.0
          Name: sepal_length, dtype: float64
```

What we get is actually a series. We can select a subset of this DataFrame, going again with the first five rows and selecting the columns `petal_length` and `species`:

```
In [15]: pd_data.head().loc[:, ['petal_length', 'species']]
```

Out[15]:

	petal_length	species
0	1.4	setosa
1	1.4	setosa
2	1.3	setosa
3	1.5	setosa
4	1.4	setosa

```
In [16]: type(pd_data.sepal_length)
```

Out[16]: pandas.core.series.Series

With that said, pandas, at its core, is built on top of NumPy. In fact, we can see the NumPy object that pandas is using to describe its contents:

```
In [17]: pd_data.values
```

```
Out[17]: array([[5.1, 3.5, 1.4, 0.2, 'setosa'],
               [4.9, 3.0, 1.4, 0.2, 'setosa'],
               [4.7, 3.2, 1.3, 0.2, 'setosa'],
               [4.6, 3.1, 1.5, 0.2, 'setosa'],
               [5.0, 3.6, 1.4, 0.2, 'setosa'],
               [5.4, 3.9, 1.7, 0.4, 'setosa'],
               [4.6, 3.4, 1.4, 0.3, 'setosa'],
               [5.0, 3.4, 1.5, 0.2, 'setosa'],
               [4.4, 2.9, 1.4, 0.2, 'setosa'],
               [4.9, 3.1, 1.5, 0.1, 'setosa'],
               [5.4, 3.7, 1.5, 0.2, 'setosa'],
               [4.8, 3.4, 1.6, 0.2, 'setosa'],
               [4.8, 3.0, 1.4, 0.1, 'setosa'],
               [4.3, 3.0, 1.1, 0.1, 'setosa'],
               [5.8, 4.0, 1.2, 0.2, 'setosa'],
               [5.7, 4.4, 1.5, 0.4, 'setosa'],
               [5.4, 3.9, 1.3, 0.4, 'setosa'],
               [5.1, 3.5, 1.4, 0.3, 'setosa'],
               [5.7, 3.8, 1.7, 0.3, 'setosa'],
```

And in fact, that NumPy object we created earlier can be used to construct a pandas DataFrame:

```
In [18]:  np_pd_data = pd.DataFrame(np_data)    # Converting to a DataFrame
          np_pd_data

Out[18]:
```

	sepal_length	sepal_width	petal_length	petal_width	species
0	5.101562	3.500000	1.400391	0.199951	setosa
1	4.898438	3.000000	1.400391	0.199951	setosa
2	4.699219	3.199219	1.299805	0.199951	setosa
3	4.601562	3.099609	1.500000	0.199951	setosa
4	5.000000	3.599609	1.400391	0.199951	setosa
5	5.398438	3.900391	1.700195	0.399902	setosa
6	4.601562	3.400391	1.400391	0.300049	setosa
7	5.000000	3.400391	1.500000	0.199951	setosa
8	4.398438	2.900391	1.400391	0.199951	setosa
9	4.898438	3.099609	1.500000	0.099976	setosa
10	5.398438	3.699219	1.500000	0.199951	setosa

Now it's time to take a good look at pandas series and DataFrames.

Exploring series and DataFrame objects

We'll start looking at pandas series and DataFrame objects. In this section, we'll start getting familiar with pandas series and DataFrames by looking at how they are created. We'll start with series since they are the building block of DataFrames. Series are one-dimensional array-like objects containing data of a single type. From this fact alone, you'd rightly conclude that they're very similar to one-dimensional NumPy arrays, but series have different methods than NumPy arrays that make them more ideal for managing data. They can be created with an index, which is metadata identifying the contents of the series. Series can handle missing data; they do so by representing missing data with NumPy's NaN.

Creating series

We can create series from array-like objects; these include lists, tuples, and NumPy `ndarray` objects. We can also create a series from a Python dict. Another way to add an index to a series is to create one by passing either an index or an array-like object of unique hashable values to the index argument of the create method for the series.

We can also create an index separately. Creating an index is a lot like creating a series, but we require all values to be unique. Every series has an index; if we do not assign an index, then a simple numeric sequence starting from 0 will be used as the index. We can give a series a name by passing a string to the name argument of the series' create method. We do this so that, if we were to create a DataFrame using this series, we can automatically assign a column or row name to the series, and so we can tell what date the series is describing.

In other words, the name provides useful metadata, and I would recommend setting this argument whenever possible, within reason. Let's see a working example. Notice that we import the series and DataFrame objects directly into the namespace:

```
In [1]:  import pandas as pd
         from pandas import Series, DataFrame
         import numpy as np
```

We do this very frequently because these objects are used exhaustively. Here, we create two series, one consisting of the numbers 1, 2, 3, 4, and another consisting of the letters a, b, and c:

```
In [2]:  ser1 = Series([1, 2, 3, 4])
         ser2 = Series(['a', 'b', 'c'])
         print(ser1)

         0    1
         1    2
         2    3
         3    4
         dtype: int64

In [3]:  print(ser2)

         0    a
         1    b
         2    c
         dtype: object
```

Notice that an index was automatically assigned to both of these series.

Let's create an index; this index consists of names of cities in the United States:

```
In [4]:  # Create a pandas Index
         idx = pd.Index(["New York", "Los Angeles", "Chicago",
                         "Houston", "Philadelphia", "Phoenix", "San Antonio",
                         "San Diego", "Dallas"])
         print(idx)

         Index(['New York', 'Los Angeles', 'Chicago', 'Houston', 'Philadelphia',
                'Phoenix', 'San Antonio', 'San Diego', 'Dallas'],
               dtype='object')
```

We are going to create a new series consisting of numbers called `pops`, and we will assign this index to the series we created. The population of these cities is in thousands. I got this data from Wikipedia. We also assign the name `Population` to this series. This is the result:

```
In [5]:  pops = Series([8550, 3972, 2721, 2296, 1567, np.nan, 1470, 1395, 1300],
                        index=idx, name="Population")
         print(pops)

         New York         8550.0
         Los Angeles      3972.0
         Chicago          2721.0
         Houston          2296.0
         Philadelphia     1567.0
         Phoenix             NaN
         San Antonio      1470.0
         San Diego        1395.0
         Dallas           1300.0
         Name: Population, dtype: float64
```

Notice that I inserted a missing value; this is the population of `Phoenix`, which we do know, but I felt like adding a little extra just to demonstrate. We can also create a series using a dictionary. In this case, the keys of the dictionary are going to be the index of the resulting series, and the values will be the values of the resulting series. So here, we add `state` names:

```
In [6]: state = Series({"New York": "New York", "Los Angeles": "California", "Phoenix": "Arizona", "San Antonio": "Texas",
                "San Diego": "California", "Dallas": "Texas"}, name = "State")
        print(state)

        Dallas              Texas
        Los Angeles     California
        New York          New York
        Phoenix            Arizona
        San Antonio          Texas
        San Diego       California
        Name: State, dtype: object
```

I also create a series using a dictionary and I populate it with the areas of these respective cities:

```
In [7]: area = Series({"New York": 302.6, "Los Angeles": 468.7, "Philadelphia": 134.1, "Phoenix": 516.7, "Austin": 322.48},
                name = "Area")
        print(area)

        Austin          322.48
        Los Angeles     468.70
        New York        302.60
        Philadelphia    134.10
        Phoenix         516.70
        Name: Area, dtype: float64
```

Now I would like to draw your attention to the fact that these series are not of equal length, and furthermore they don't all contain the same keys. They don't all contain the same indices. We're going to use these series later, so keep this in mind.

Creating DataFrames

Series are interesting, primarily because they are used to build pandas DataFrames. We can think of a pandas DataFrame as combining series together to form a tabular object, with rows and columns being the series. We can create DataFrames in a variety of ways and we will be demonstrating some here. We can give a DataFrame an index. We can also manually specify the names of columns by setting the columns argument. Choosing column names follows the same rules as choosing index names.

Let's see some of the ways we can create DataFrames. The first thing we will do is create DataFrames, and we are not going to care too much about their indices. We can create a DataFrame from a NumPy array:

```
In [8]:  # From a NumPy array
         mat = np.arange(0,9).reshape(3, 3)
         print(mat)

         [[0 1 2]
          [3 4 5]
          [6 7 8]]
```

Here, we have a three-dimensional NumPy array populated with numbers. We can simply create a DataFrame from this object by passing this object as the first argument to the DataFrame creation function:

```
In [9]:  print(DataFrame(mat))

                 0   1   2
          0   0   1   2
          1   3   4   5
          2   6   7   8
```

If we want to, we can add indices and column names to this DataFrame:

```
In [10]:  # Adding labels
          print(DataFrame(mat, index=['a', 'b', 'c'], columns = ['alpha', 'beta', 'gamma']))

              alpha  beta  gamma
          a      0     1      2
          b      3     4      5
          c      6     7      8
```

We create DataFrames from a list of tuples:

```
In [11]:   # What amounts to a 2D array (each tuple a row)
           arr = [(1, 'a'), (2, 'b'), (3, 'c')]
           print(arr)

           [(1, 'a'), (2, 'b'), (3, 'c')]

In [12]:   print(DataFrame(arr, columns = ["Numbers", "Letters"]))

                 Numbers Letters
           0         1       a
           1         2       b
           2         3       c
```

We can also create DataFrames from a `dict`:

```
In [13]:   # Creating from a dict
           print(DataFrame({"Numbers": [1, 2, 3], "Letters": ['a', 'b', 'c']}))

               Letters  Numbers
           0      a        1
           1      b        2
           2      c        3
```

Now, suppose we want to create a DataFrame and we pass it a dict, but the dict does not consist of lists that are all of the same length. This will produce an error:

```
In [14]:   # What if not all lists are the same length?
           # We get an error
           print(DataFrame({"Numbers": [1, 2, 3, 4], "Letters": ['a', 'b', 'c']}))

           ----------------------------------------------------------------------
           ValueError                                Traceback (most recent call last)
           <ipython-input-14-51586e2e56fe> in <module>()
                 1 # What if not all lists are the same length?
                 2 # We get an error
           ----> 3 print(DataFrame({"Numbers": [1, 2, 3, 4], "Letters": ['a', 'b', 'c']}))
```

The reason is that an index will need to be assigned to these values, but the function does not know how to assign missing information. It does not know how to align the data in these lists.

However, if we were to pass a dictionary (and the values of the dictionary are series of unequal lengths but these series have an index), it would not produce an error:

```
In [15]:  # Do we get an error?
          DataFrame({"Numbers": ser1, "Letters": ser2})

Out[15]:
```

	Letters	Numbers
0	a	1
1	b	2
2	c	3
3	NaN	4

Instead, since it knows how to line up elements in the different series, it will do so and fill in any spots where information is missing with NaN.

Now let's create a DataFrame that contains information about series, and you may recall that these series are not of the same length. Furthermore, they don't all contain the same index values, and yet we are able to create a DataFrame from them:

```
In [16]:  # When passed as a list, series are treated as rows
          # Notice that these Series are not the same length nor all have the same entries; nan will be generated
          print(DataFrame([pops, state, area]))

                      Austin  Chicago Dallas  Houston Los Angeles  New York  \
          Population     NaN   2721.0   1300   2296.0        3972      8550
          State          NaN      NaN  Texas      NaN  California  New York
          Area        322.48      NaN    NaN      NaN       468.7     302.6

                      Philadelphia  Phoenix San Antonio  San Diego
          Population        1567.0      NaN       1470       1395
          State                NaN  Arizona      Texas  California
          Area               134.1    516.7        NaN        NaN
```

However, in this situation, this is not the DataFrame that we want. It is of the wrong orientation; the rows are what we would interpret as variables, and the columns are what we would interpret as keys. So, we can create the DataFrame using a dictionary in the method that we actually want:

```
In [17]:  print(DataFrame({"Population": pops, "State": state, "Area": area}))

                        Area  Population         State
          Austin      322.48         NaN           NaN
          Chicago        NaN      2721.0           NaN
          Dallas         NaN      1300.0         Texas
          Houston        NaN      2296.0           NaN
          Los Angeles 468.70      3972.0    California
          New York    302.60      8550.0      New York
          Philadelphia 134.10     1567.0           NaN
          Phoenix     516.70         NaN       Arizona
          San Antonio    NaN      1470.0         Texas
          San Diego      NaN      1395.0    California
```

Or we can use the transpose method, the T method, as with a NumPy array, to get the DataFrame into the proper orientation:

```
In [18]:  # Or, we could use DataFrame's T (transpose) method
          print(DataFrame([pops, state, area]).T)

                       Population       State   Area
          Austin              NaN         NaN 322.48
          Chicago            2721         NaN    NaN
          Dallas             1300       Texas    NaN
          Houston            2296         NaN    NaN
          Los Angeles        3972  California  468.7
          New York           8550    New York  302.6
          Philadelphia       1567         NaN  134.1
          Phoenix             NaN     Arizona  516.7
          San Antonio        1470       Texas    NaN
          San Diego          1395  California    NaN
```

Adding data

After creating a series or DataFrame, we can add more data to it using the `concat` function or `append` method. We pass an object to the method containing the data that will be added to the existing object. If we are working with a DataFrame, we may be able to append new rows or new columns. We can add new columns with the `concat` function, and use a `dict`, a series, or DataFrame for concatenating.

Let's see how we can add new information to the series or DataFrame. Let's, for example, add two new cities to the `pops` series, for `Seattle` and `Denver`. This is the result:

```
In [19]:  # Let's append new data to each Series
          pops.append(Series({"Seattle": 684, "Denver": 683}))    # Not done in place

Out[19]:  New York        8550.0
          Los Angeles     3972.0
          Chicago         2721.0
          Houston         2296.0
          Philadelphia    1567.0
          Phoenix            NaN
          San Antonio     1470.0
          San Diego       1395.0
          Dallas          1300.0
          Denver           683.0
          Seattle          684.0
          dtype: float64
```

Notice that this was not done in place; that is, a new series was returned rather than changing the existing series. And I'm going to append new rows to this DataFrame by creating a DataFrame with the data that I want:

```
In [20]: df = DataFrame([pops, state, area]).T
         df.append(DataFrame({"Population": Series({"Seattle": 684, "Denver": 683}),
                              "State": Series({"Seattle": "Washington", "Denver": "Colorado"}),
                              "Area": Series({"Seattle": np.nan, "Denver": np.nan})}))
```

Out[20]:

	Area	Population	State
Austin	322.48	NaN	NaN
Chicago	NaN	2721	NaN
Dallas	NaN	1300	Texas
Houston	NaN	2296	NaN
Los Angeles	468.7	3972	California
New York	302.6	8550	New York
Philadelphia	134.1	1567	NaN
Phoenix	516.7	NaN	Arizona
San Antonio	NaN	1470	Texas
San Diego	NaN	1395	California
Denver	NaN	683	Colorado
Seattle	NaN	684	Washington

I can also add new columns to this DataFrame by effectively creating multiple DataFrames.

I have a list, and in this list I have two DataFrames. I have `df`, and I have the new DataFrame containing the columns that I wish to add. This will not change the existing DataFrames, but instead it will create a brand new DataFrame, which we then need to assign to a variable:

```
In [21]: pd.concat([df, DataFrame({"Numbers": Series(np.arange(9), index=pops.index),
                                    "Letters": Series(['a', 'c', 'd', 'h', 'l', 'n', 'p', 'p', 's'], index=pops.index)})],
             axis=1)
```

```
Out[21]:
```

	Population	State	Area	Letters	Numbers
Austin	NaN	NaN	322.48	NaN	NaN
Chicago	2721	NaN	NaN	d	2.0
Dallas	1300	Texas	NaN	s	8.0
Houston	2296	NaN	NaN	h	3.0
Los Angeles	3972	California	468.7	c	1.0
New York	8550	New York	302.6	a	0.0
Philadelphia	1567	NaN	134.1	l	4.0
Phoenix	NaN	Arizona	516.7	n	5.0
San Antonio	1470	Texas	NaN	p	6.0
San Diego	1395	California	NaN	p	7.0

Saving DataFrames

Suppose we have a DataFrame; call it df. We can easily save the DataFrame's data. We can pickle the DataFrame (which saves it in a format commonly used in Python) with the to_pickle method, passing the filename as the first parameter.

We can save a CSV file with to_csv, a JSON file with to_json, or an HTML table with to_html. Many other formats are available; for example, we can save data in Excel spreadsheets, Stata, DAT files, HDF5 format, and SQL commands to insert it into a database, even copied to your clipboard.

We may discuss other methods along with how to load data in different formats later.

In this example, I save the data in the DataFrame to a CSV file:

```
In [22]: df = DataFrame([pops, state, area]).T
         # Saving data to csv file
         df.to_csv("cities.csv")
```

Hopefully, by now, you are more familiar with what series and DataFrames are. Next, we will talk about subsetting data in a DataFrame so that you can get the information you need fast and easily.

Subsetting your data

Now that we can make pandas series and DataFrames, let's work with the data they contain. In this section, we will see how to get and manipulate the data we store in a pandas series or DataFrame. Naturally, this is an important topic; these objects will be useless otherwise.

You should not be surprised that there are many variations on how to subset DataFrames. We will not cover every idiosyncrasy here; refer to the documentation for an exhaustive discussion. But we will discuss the most important functionality every user of pandas should be aware of.

Subsetting a series

Let's first look at series. Since they are similar to DataFrames, there are key lessons that apply there. The simplest way to subset a series is with square brackets, and we can do so as we would subset a list or NumPy array. The colon operator does work here, but there's more that we can do. We can select elements based on the index of the series, as opposed to just the position of the elements in the series, following many of the same rules as if we were working with integers indicating the position of elements in the series.

The colon operator also works, and largely as expected. Select all elements between two indices:

```
In [3]:   srs = Series(np.arange(5),
                        index=["alpha", "beta", "gamma", "delta", "epsilon"])
          srs

Out[3]:   alpha      0
          beta       1
          gamma      2
          delta      3
          epsilon    4
          dtype: int32
```

But unlike working with integer positions, the colon operator does include the endpoint. A particularly interesting case is when indexing with Booleans. I'll show what such a use might may look like. This can be handy to get data in a particular range. If we can get an array-like object, such as a list, NumPy array, or another series, to produce Booleans, this object can be used for indexing. Here is some example code demonstrating indexing a series:

```
In [4]:   srs[:2]

Out[4]:   alpha    0
          beta     1
          dtype: int32


In [5]:   srs[["beta", "delta"]]

Out[5]:   beta     1
          delta    3
          dtype: int32


In [6]:   srs["beta":"delta"]        # Select everything BETWEEN (and
                                     # including) beta and delta

Out[6]:   beta     1
          gamma    2
          delta    3
          dtype: int32
```

So far, integer indexing behaves as expected, along with indexing with Booleans:

```
In [7]:   srs[srs > 3]     # Select elements of srs greater than 3

Out[7]:   epsilon    4
          dtype: int32


In [8]:   srs > 3     # A look at the indexing object

Out[8]:   alpha      False
          beta       False
          gamma      False
          delta      False
          epsilon     True
          dtype: bool
```

The only really interesting example is when we use the colon operator with indices; notice that all betas and delta are included, deltas in particular. This is unlike the behavior we normally associate with the colon operator. Here is an interesting example:

```
In [9]:  srs2 = Series(["zero", "one", "two", "three", "four"],
                        index=[3, 2, 4, 0, 1])

         srs2

Out[9]:  3       zero
         2        one
         4        two
         0      three
         1       four
         dtype: object
```

We have a series, and that series has an `index` of integers that is not in order from 0 to 4, as would be typical. Now, the order is mixed up. Consider the indexing we requested. What will happen? On the one hand, we may say that the last command will select based on the indices. So it will select elements 2 and 4; there is nothing between them. But on the other hand, it might use the integer positions to select the third and fourth elements of the series. In other words, it's positions 2 and position 3 when we count from 0, as you would expect if you were to treat `srs2` as a list. Which behavior will prevail? It's not all that clear.

Indexing methods

pandas provides methods that allow us to clearly state how we want to index. We can also distinguish between indexing based on values of the index of the series, and indexing based on the position of objects in the series, as would be the case if we were working with a list. The two methods we'll focus on are `loc` and `iloc`. `loc` focuses on selecting based on the index of the series, and if we try to select key elements that don't exist, we will get an error. `iloc` indexes as if we were working with a Python list; that is, it indexes based on integer position. So, if we were to try to index with a non-integer in `iloc`, or try to select an element outside of the range of valid integers, an error will be produced. There is a `hybrid` method, `ix`, that acts like `loc`, but if passed input that cannot be interpreted with respect to the index, it will act like `iloc`. Because of the ambiguity about how `ix` will behave, I recommend sticking with `loc` or `iloc` most of the time.

Let's return to our example. It turns out that square brackets, in this case, index like `iloc`; that is, they index based on integer position as if `srs2` were a list. If we wanted to index based on the index of `srs2`, we could use `loc` to do so, getting the other possible result. Again, notice that in this case, both endpoints were included. This is unlike the behavior we normally associate with the colon operator:

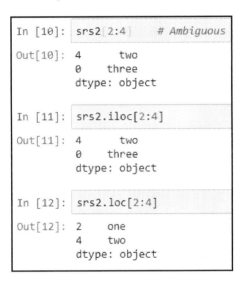

```
In [10]:  srs2[2:4]      # Ambiguous

Out[10]:  4        two
          0        three
          dtype: object

In [11]:  srs2.iloc[2:4]

Out[11]:  4        two
          0        three
          dtype: object

In [12]:  srs2.loc[2:4]

Out[12]:  2        one
          4        two
          dtype: object
```

Slicing a DataFrame

Having discussed slicing a series, let's talk about slicing a DataFrame. The good news is that, in talking about series slicing, a lot of the hard work is already done. We introduced `loc` and `iloc` as series methods, but they are DataFrame methods as well. After all, you should be thinking of DataFrames as multiple series glued together as columns.

We now need to think about how what we learned for series translates to a two-dimensional setting. If we use bracket notation, it will work only for the columns of the DataFrame. We will need to use `loc` and `iloc` to subset rows of the DataFrame. In truth, these methods can accept two positional arguments. The first positional argument determines which rows to select, and the second positional argument determines which columns to select, according to the rules we described earlier. The second argument can be emitted to select all columns and apply selection rules only to rows. This means that we should have the first argument as a colon, in order to be more choosy in the columns we select.

`loc` and `iloc` will impose index-based or integer-position-based indexing on both their arguments, while `ix` may allow for mixing of this behavior. I would not recommend doing this. The result to a later reader is too ambiguous. If you want to mix the behavior of `loc` and `iloc`, I would recommend method chaining. That is, if you want to select rows based on the index and columns based on integer locations, first use the `loc` method to choose the rows and `iloc` to choose the columns. There is no ambiguity about how elements of the DataFrame are chosen when you do this.

What if you want to choose just one column? The result is as follows:

```
In [13]: df = DataFrame(np.arange(21).reshape(7, 3),
                        columns=['AAA', 'BBB', 'CCC'],
                        index=["alpha", "beta", "gamma", "delta",
                               "epsilon", "zeta", "eta"])
         df
```

Out[13]:

	AAA	BBB	CCC
alpha	0	1	2
beta	3	4	5
gamma	6	7	8
delta	9	10	11
epsilon	12	13	14
zeta	15	16	17
eta	18	19	20

There is a shorthand for doing this; just treat the particular column as an attribute of the DataFrame, as an object, effectively selecting it using dot notation. This can be convenient:

```
In [14]: df.AAA
```

```
Out[14]: alpha      0
         beta       3
         gamma      6
         delta      9
         epsilon    12
         zeta       15
         eta        18
         Name: AAA, dtype: int32
```

Remember that pandas is built from NumPy, and behind a DataFrame are NumPy arrays.

Thus, knowing what you now know about NumPy arrays, the following fact should be no surprise to you. When assigning the result of a slicing operation of a DataFrame to a variable, what the variable hosts is not a copy of the data but a view of the data in the original DataFrame:

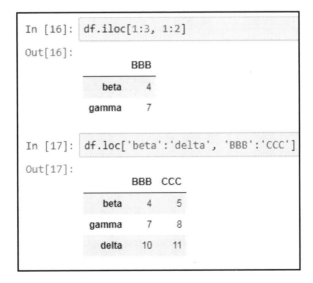

If you want to make an independent copy of this data, you will need to use the `copy` method of a DataFrame. The same holds true for series.

Let's now look at an an example. Here, we create a DataFrame, `df`, with interesting indices and column names:

```
In [18]: df.iloc[:, 1:3]
Out[18]:
                  BBB   CCC
         alpha     1     2
          beta     4     5
         gamma     7     8
         delta    10    11
       epsilon    13    14
          zeta    16    17
           eta    19    20
```

I can easily get a series representing the data in the first column, by treating the name of the first column as an attribute of `df`. Next, we see the behavior of `loc` and `iloc`. `loc` chooses rows and columns based on their indices, but `iloc` chooses them as if they were lists; that is, it uses integer positions:

```
In [19]: df.iloc[:, 1:3].loc[['alpha', 'gamma', 'zeta']]    # Mixing
Out[19]:
                BBB   CCC
       alpha     1     2
       gamma     7     8
        zeta    16    17
```

Here, we see method chaining. For input 10, you may notice that it starts like input 9 on the previous slide, but then I called `loc` on the resulting view to further subset the data. I saved the result of this method chaining in `df2`. I also changed the contents of the second column with `df2`, replacing them with a new series of custom data:

```
In [20]: df2 = df.iloc[:, 1:3].loc[['alpha', 'gamma', 'zeta']].copy()

         df2
```

Out[20]:

	BBB	CCC
alpha	1	2
gamma	7	8
zeta	16	17

Because df2 is an independent copy of df, notice that we had to use a copy method when creating df2; the original data is not affected. This gets us to an important point. Series and DataFrames are not immutable objects; you can change their contents. This works similarly to making changes to content in NumPy arrays. Be careful when making changes across columns though; they may not be of the same data type, leading to unpredictable results sometimes:

```
In [21]: df2['CCC'] = Series({'alpha': 11, 'gamma': 18, 'zeta': 5})

         df2
```

Out[21]:

	BBB	CCC
alpha	1	11
gamma	7	18
zeta	16	5

We see what assignment looks like here:

```
In [22]: df2.iloc[1, 1] = 2
         df2
```

Out[22]:

	BBB	CCC
alpha	1	11
gamma	7	2
zeta	16	5

This behavior is pretty similar to what you've seen in NumPy, so I won't discuss it much. There's more to be said about subsetting, in particular when the index is actually a `MultiIndex`, but this is for later.

Summary

In this chapter, we introduced pandas and looked at what it does; we explored pandas series, DataFrames, and creating them. We also looked at adding data to a series and a DataFrame; finally we covered saving DataFrames. In the next chapter, we will talk about arithmetic, function applications, and function mapping.

5
Arithmetic, Function Application, and Mapping with pandas

We've seen some basic tasks done with pandas series and DataFrames. Let's move on to more interesting applications. In this chapter, we'll revisit some topics discussed previously, regarding applying functions in arithmetic to a multivariate object and handling missing data in pandas.

Arithmetic

Let's see an example. The first thing we'll do is start up pandas and NumPy.

In the following screenshot, we have two series, srs1 and srs2:

```
In [1]:  import pandas as pd
         from pandas import Series, DataFrame
         import numpy as np

         srs1 = Series([1, 9, -4, 3, 3])
         srs2 = Series([2, 3, 4, 5, 10], index=[0, 1, 2, 3, 5])
         print(srs1)

         0    1
         1    9
         2    -4
         3    3
         4    3
         dtype: int64

In [2]:  print(srs2)

         0     2
         1     3
         2     4
         3     5
         5    10
         dtype: int64
```

srs1 has an index that goes from 0 to 4, whereas srs2 has an index that goes from 0 to 3, skips 4, and then goes to 5. These two series are technically the same length, but that doesn't necessarily mean that the elements will match up as you might expect. For example, let's consider the following code. What happens when we add srs1 and srs2?

```
In [3]:  srs1 + srs2

Out[3]:  0     3.0
         1    12.0
         2     0.0
         3     8.0
         4     NaN
         5     NaN
         dtype: float64
```

Two NaNs were produced. That was because, for elements 0 to 3, there were elements in both series that could be matched up, but for 4 and 5, there were non-equivalent elements for each index in both series. This is also going to be the case when we multiply, shown as follows:

```
In [4]:  srs1 * srs2

Out[4]:  0      2.0
         1     27.0
         2    -16.0
         3     15.0
         4      NaN
         5      NaN
         dtype: float64
```

Or if we were to exponentiate, as follows:

```
In [5]:  srs1 ** srs2

Out[5]:  0      1.0
         1    729.0
         2    256.0
         3    243.0
         4      NaN
         5      NaN
         dtype: float64
```

That being said, Boolean arithmetic is different. In this case, comparison is done element by element, as you would normally expect. In fact, it seems that Boolean comparison doesn't care at all about the index, shown as follows:

```
                srs1 > srs2

Out[6]:  0      False
         1      True
         2      False
         3      False
         4      False
         dtype: bool


In [7]:  srs1 <= srs2     # Opposite of above

Out[7]:  0      True
         1      False
         2      True
         3      True
         4      True
         dtype: bool
```

```
In [8]:  srs1 > Series([1, 2, 3, 4, 5], index = [4, 3, 2, 1, 0])

Out[8]:  0      False
         1      True
         2      False
         3      False
         4      False
         dtype: bool
```

Take the square root of `srs2`, shown here:

```
In [9]:  np.sqrt(srs2)

Out[9]:  0      1.414214
         1      1.732051
         2      2.000000
         3      2.236068
         5      3.162278
         dtype: float64
```

Notice that the indices of the series were preserved, but we have taken the square roots of the elements in the series. Let's take the absolute value of `srs1`—again an expected result—and notice that we can confirm that this is still in fact a series, shown as follows:

```
In [10]: np.abs(srs1)

Out[10]: 0    1
         1    9
         2    4
         3    3
         4    3
         dtype: int64

In [11]: type(np.abs(srs1))

Out[11]: pandas.core.series.Series
```

Now, let's apply a custom `ufunc`. Here, we're using decorator notation. In the next screenshot, let's see what happens when we use a vectorized version of this truncation function, an array, and then when we apply it to `srs1`, shown as follows:

```
In [12]: # Define a cusom ufunc: notice the decorator notation?
         @np.vectorize
         def trunc(x):
             return x if x > 0 else 0

         trunc(np.array([-1, 5, 4, -3, 0]))

Out[12]: array([0, 5, 4, 0, 0])

In [13]: trunc(srs1)

Out[13]: array([1, 9, 0, 3, 3], dtype=int64)
```

Notice that `srs1`, which used to be a pandas series, is no longer a series; it is now a NumPy `ndarray`. So, the index that the series had was lost.

Compute the mean of `srs1`:

```
In [15]:   # Mean of a series
           srs1.mean()

Out[15]:   2.4
```

Or a standard deviation, as follows:

```
In [16]:   srs1.std()

Out[16]:   4.669047011971501
```

The maximal element, as follows:

```
In [17]:   srs1.max()

Out[17]:   9
```

Or where the maximal element is located, as follows:

```
In [18]:   srs1.argmax()    # Returns the index where the maximum is

Out[18]:   1
```

Or the cumulative sum, elements of the series in succession to create a new series:

```
In [19]:   srs1.cumsum()

Out[19]:   0       1
           1       10
           2       6
           3       9
           4       12
           dtype: int64
```

```
In [20]:  srs1.abs()      # An alternative to the abs function in NumPy

Out[20]:  0    1
          1    9
          2    4
          3    3
          4    3
          dtype: int64
```

Now, let's talk about function application and mapping. This is similar to the truncation function we defined before. I'm using a `lambda` expression to create a temporary function that will then be applied to every element of `srs1`, shown as follows:

```
In [21]:  srs1.apply(lambda x: x if x > 2 else 2)

Out[21]:  0    2
          1    9
          2    2
          3    3
          4    3
          dtype: int64
```

We could have defined a vectorized function to do this, but notice that by using apply, we managed to preserve the series structure. Let's create a new series, `srs3`, shown as follows:

```
In [22]:  srs3 = Series(['alpha', 'beta', 'gamma', 'delta'], index = ['a', 'b', 'c', 'd'])
          print(srs3)

          a    alpha
          b     beta
          c    gamma
          d    delta
          dtype: object
```

Let's see what happens when we have a dictionary and then map `srs3` to the dictionary. Notice that the elements of `srs3` correspond to the keys of the dictionary. So, when we map, what I end up with is another series and the values of the dictionary objects that correspond to the keys looked up by the series map, shown as follows:

```
In [23]:   obj = {"alpha": 1, "beta": 2, "gamma": -1, "delta": -3}
           srs3.map(obj)

Out[23]:   a     1
           b     2
           c    -1
           d    -3
           dtype: int64
```

This also works with functions, like how apply does.

Arithmetic with DataFrames

Arithmetic between DataFrames bears some similarity with series or NumPy array arithmetic. Arithmetic between two DataFrames, or a DataFrame and a scaler, works as you'd expect; but arithmetic between a DataFrame and a series requires care. What must be kept in mind is that arithmetic involving a DataFrame applies to the columns of the DataFrame first, and then it applies across the rows of the DataFrame. So, columns in the DataFrame will be matched with either the single scalar, elements of the series with indices of the same name as the columns, or columns in the other involved DataFrame. If there are elements of either the series or either DataFrame that cannot find a mate, then new columns will be generated, corresponding to the unmatched elements or columns and populated with Nan.

Vectorization with DataFrames

Vectorization can be applied to DataFrames. Many NumPy `ufuncs`, such as square root or `sqrt`, will work as expected when given a DataFrame; in fact, they may still return a DataFrame when given a DataFrame. That said, this cannot be guaranteed, especially when using a custom `ufunc` created with vectorize. They may instead return an `ndarray` in such a situation. While these methods work on DataFrames with common data types, it cannot be guaranteed that they will work on all DataFrames.

DataFrame function application

Not surprisingly, DataFrames provide methods for function application. There are two methods you should be aware of, `apply` and `applymap`. `apply` takes a function and, by default, applies the function to the series corresponding to each column of the DataFrame. What is produced depends on what the function does. We can change the axis argument of apply so that instead of applying to columns (that is, across rows), it applies to rows (that is, across columns). `applymap` has a different purpose than apply. Whereas apply will evaluate the supplied function on each column and thus should be prepared to take a series, `applymap` will evaluate the `pass` function on each element of the DataFrame individually.

We could `apply` functions to get the quantities we want, but it's often more useful and perhaps faster to use existing methods provided with DataFrames.

Let's see some demonstrations of working with DataFrames. Many of the tricks that worked with series will also work with DataFrames but with a slight complication. So let's first create a DataFrame, shown as follows:

```
In [27]: df = DataFrame(np.arange(15).reshape(5, 3), columns=["AAA", "BBB", "CCC"])
         print(df)

            AAA  BBB  CCC
         0    0    1    2
         1    3    4    5
         2    6    7    8
         3    9   10   11
         4   12   13   14
```

Here we subtract a DataFrame from another DataFrame:

```
In [28]:  # Should get 0's, and CCC gets NaN because no match
          df - df.loc[:,["AAA", "BBB"]]
```

Out[28]:

	AAA	BBB	CCC
0	0	0	NaN
1	0	0	NaN
2	0	0	NaN
3	0	0	NaN
4	0	0	NaN

There are also useful methods for working with DataFrames; for example, we can take the mean of each column, shown here:

```
In [29]:  df.mean()

Out[29]:  AAA      6.0
          BBB      7.0
          CCC      8.0
          dtype: float64
```

Or we can find each column's standard deviation, shown here:

```
In [30]:  df.std()

Out[30]:  AAA      4.743416
          BBB      4.743416
          CCC      4.743416
          dtype: float64
```

Another useful trick would be to standardize the numbers in each column. Now, `df.mean` and `df.std` return a series, so what we're actually doing is subtracting a series and then dividing by a series, shown as follows:

```
In [31]:  # This is known as standardizatic
          (df - df.mean())/df.std()
```

Out[31]:

	AAA	BBB	CCC
0	-1.264911	-1.264911	-1.264911
1	-0.632456	-0.632456	-0.632456
2	0.000000	0.000000	0.000000
3	0.632456	0.632456	0.632456
4	1.264911	1.264911	1.264911

Let's now look at some vectorization. The square root function, which is a vectorized function from NumPy, works as expected on the DataFrame:

```
In [32]:  np.sqrt(df)
```

Out[32]:

	AAA	BBB	CCC
0	0.000000	1.000000	1.414214
1	1.732051	2.000000	2.236068
2	2.449490	2.645751	2.828427
3	3.000000	3.162278	3.316625
4	3.464102	3.605551	3.741657

Remember the custom `ufunctrunk`? It will not give us a DataFrame, but it will evaluate and return something that is DataFrame-like, shown as follows:

```
In [33]:  # trunc is a custom ufunc: does not give a DataFrame
          trunc(df)

Out[33]:  array([[ 0,  1,  2],
                 [ 3,  4,  5],
                 [ 6,  7,  8],
                 [ 9, 10, 11],
                 [12, 13, 14]])
```

However, this is going to produce an error when run on a DataFrame of mixed data types:

```
In [34]:  # Mixed data
          df2 = DataFrame({"AAA": [1, 2, 3, 4], "BBB": [0, -9, 9, 3], "CCC": ["Bob", "Terry", "Matt", "Simon"]})
          print(df2)

             AAA  BBB    CCC
          0    1    0    Bob
          1    2   -9  Terry
          2    3    9   Matt
          3    4    3  Simon
```

```
In [35]:  # Produces an error
          np.sqrt(df2)

          ----------------------------------------------------------------

          AttributeError                       Traceback (most recent call last)
          <ipython-input-35-1d62d738155f> in <module>()
                1 # Produces an error
          ----> 2 np.sqrt(df2)

          AttributeError: 'int' object has no attribute 'sqrt'
```

This is why you need to be careful. Now here, I'm going to show you a trick for avoiding the problem of mixed data types. Notice that I am using a method that I have not introduced before, called `select_dtypes`. What this will do is select columns that have a particular `dtype`. In this case, I am requesting columns of numeric `dtype`:

```
In [36]:  # Let's select JUST numeric data
          # The select_dtypes() method selects columns based on their dtype
          # np.number indicates numeric dtypes
          # Here we select columns only with numeric data
          df2.select_dtypes([np.number])
```

Out[36]:

	AAA	BBB
0	1	0
1	2	-9
2	3	9
3	4	3

Notice that the third column, which consists of string data, is excluded. So when I take the square root, it works just fine except for the negative number:

```
In [37]:  np.sqrt(df2.select_dtypes([np.number]))
```

Out[37]:

	AAA	BBB
0	1.000000	0.000000
1	1.414214	NaN
2	1.732051	3.000000
3	2.000000	1.732051

Now, let's look at the function's application. Here, I'm going to define a function that computes what is known as the **geometric mean**. So the first thing I do is define a geometric mean function:

```
In [38]:  # Define a function for the geometric mean
          def geomean(srs):
              return srs.prod() ** (1 / len(srs))    # prod method is product of all elements of srs

          # Demo
          geomean(Series([2, 3, 4]))
Out[38]:  2.8844991406148166
```

We apply this function to every column of the DataFrame:

```
In [39]: df.apply(geomean)

Out[39]: AAA      0.000000
         BBB      5.154900
         CCC      6.578428
         dtype: float64


In [40]: df.apply(geomean, axis='columns')

Out[40]: 0       0.000000
         1       3.914868
         2       6.952053
         3       9.966555
         4      12.974308
         dtype: float64
```

The last trick I show is with `applymap`, where I demonstrate how this function works with a new lambda for a truncation function, this time truncating at 3:

```
In [41]: # Apply a truncation function to each element of df
         df.applymap(lambda x: x if x > 3 else 3)
```

Out[41]:

	AAA	BBB	CCC
0	3	3	3
1	3	4	5
2	6	7	8
3	9	10	11
4	12	13	14

Next, we will talk about the means of addressing missing data in DataFrames.

Handling missing data in a pandas DataFrame

In this section, we will be looking at how we can handle missing data in a pandas DataFrame. We have a few ways of detecting missing data that work for both series and DataFrames. We could use NumPy's `isnan` function; we could also use the `isnull` or `notnull` method supplied with series and DataFrames for detection. NaN detection could be useful for custom approaches for handling missing information.

In this Notebook, we're going to look at ways of managing missing information. First we generate a DataFrame containing missing data, illustrated in the following screenshot:

```
In [1]: import pandas as pd
        from pandas import Series, DataFrame
        import numpy as np
        import random

        # Create a data frame of random numbers, some randomly censored
        vals = np.random.randn(21)
        vals[random.sample([i for i in range(21)], 5)] = np.nan
        df = DataFrame(vals.reshape(7, 3), columns = ["AAA", "BBB", "CCC"])
        df
```

Out[1]:

	AAA	BBB	CCC
0	-0.955540	NaN	0.740858
1	-0.630479	0.003919	NaN
2	1.161989	0.389397	0.290482
3	NaN	0.700840	0.581674
4	NaN	0.682088	1.438320
5	-2.636118	-1.049945	0.384816
6	1.972780	-0.214350	NaN

As mentioned before in pandas, missing information is encoded by NumPy's NaN. This is, obviously, not necessarily how missing information is encoded everywhere. For example, in some surveys, missing data is encoded by an impossible numeric value. Say, the number of children the mother has is 999; this is obviously not correct. This is an example of using a sentinel value to indicate missing information.

But here, we're simply going to use the pandas convention of representing missing data with NaN. We can also create a series with missing data in it. The next screenshot shows that series:

```
In [2]:  srs = Series([2, 3, 3, 9, 8, np.nan, 8, np.nan, 4, 4, 5])
         print(srs)

         0      2.0
         1      3.0
         2      3.0
         3      9.0
         4      8.0
         5      NaN
         6      8.0
         7      NaN
         8      4.0
         9      4.0
         10     5.0
         dtype: float64
```

Let's look at some methods for detecting missing data. These methods are going to produce identical results or completely contradictory results. For example, we could use NumPy's isnan function to return a DataFrame that is true where data is NaN or missing, and false otherwise:

```
In [3]:  np.isnan(df)
```

Out[3]:

	AAA	BBB	CCC
0	False	True	False
1	False	False	True
2	False	False	False
3	True	False	False
4	True	False	False
5	False	False	False
6	False	False	True

The `isnull` method does a similar thing; it's just that it uses the DataFrames method as opposed to a NumPy function, shown as follows:

```
In [4]: df.isnull()

Out[4]:
```

	AAA	BBB	CCC
0	False	True	False
1	False	False	True
2	False	False	False
3	True	False	False

The `notnull` function is basically the exact opposite of the `isnull` function; it returns false when data is missing, and true when data is not missing, shown as follows:

```
In [5]: df.notnull()    # Opposite of isnull() and isnan()

Out[5]:
```

	AAA	BBB	CCC
0	True	False	True
1	True	True	False
2	True	True	True
3	False	True	True
4	False	True	True
5	True	True	True
6	True	True	False

Deleting missing information

The `dropna` for series and DataFrames can be useful for creating a copy of the object where rows of missing information are removed. By default, it drops rows with any missing data, and when used with a series, it eliminates elements with NaN. If you want this done in place, set the `inplace` parameter to `true`.

If we only want to remove rows that contain only missing information, and thus no information of any use, we can set the how parameter to all. By default, this method works along rows, but if we want to change it to work along columns, we can set the access argument to 1.

Here's an example of what we just discussed. Let's take this DataFrame, df, and drop any rows where missing data is present:

In [6]:	df.dropna()		
Out[6]:	**AAA**	**BBB**	**CCC**
2	1.161989	0.389397	0.290482
5	-2.636118	-1.049945	0.384816

Notice that we have dramatically shrunk the size of our DataFrame; only two rows consisted only of complete information. We can do a similar thing with the series, shown as follows:

```
In [7]:  print(srs.dropna())
         0     2.0
         1     3.0
         2     3.0
         3     9.0
         4     8.0
         6     8.0
         8     4.0
         9     4.0
         10    5.0
         dtype: float64
```

Sometimes, missing information is simply ignored when computing some metrics. For example, it's not at all problematic to simply exclude missing information when computing particular metrics such as mean, sum, standard deviation, and so on. This is done by default by many pandas methods, though it is possible to change parameters to control this behavior, perhaps specified by a parameter like skipna. This approach may be a good intermediate step when we are trying to fill in missing data. For example, we may try to fill missing data in a column with the mean of the non-missing data.

Filling missing information

We can use the `fillna` method to replace missing information in a series or DataFrame. We give `fillna` an object instructing the method how this information should be replaced. By default, the method creates a new DataFrame or series. We can give `fillna` a single value, a `dict`, a series, or a DataFrame. If given a single value, then all entries indicating missing information will be replaced with that value. A `dict` can be used for more advanced replacement schemes. The values of the `dict` could correspond to, say, columns of the DataFrame; think of it as telling how to fill missing information in each column. If a series is used for filling missing information in a series, then the past series tells how to fill particular entries in the series with the missing data. This holds analogously when a DataFrame is used for filling missing information in a DataFrame.

If a series is used for filling missing information in a DataFrame, then the series index should correspond to columns of the DataFrame, and it gives values for filling particular columns in that DataFrame.

Let's look at some of the approaches to filling in missing information. For example, we may try to fill in missing information by computing the mean of the rest of the dataset, and then filling in missing data in that dataset with the mean. In the next screenshot, we can see filling in missing information with zeros, which is a very crude approach:

```
In [8]:  xbar = srs.mean()      # By default, ignores nan
         print(xbar)

         5.111111111111111


In [9]:  print(srs.fillna(0))

         0      2.0
         1      3.0
         2      3.0
         3      9.0
         4      8.0
         5      0.0
         6      8.0
         7      0.0
         8      4.0
         9      4.0
         10     5.0
         dtype: float64
```

A slightly better approach would be to fill in missing data with its mean, shown as follows:

```
In [10]: print(srs.fillna(xbar))
         0    2.000000
         1    3.000000
         2    3.000000
         3    9.000000
         4    8.000000
         5    5.111111
         6    8.000000
```

But notice that some things may not be the same. For example, while the mean of the new dataset with missing information filled in has the same mean as the original dataset, compare the standard deviation of the original dataset to the standard deviation of the new dataset, shown as follows:

```
In [11]: # How does the mean of this data compare to before?
         srs.fillna(xbar).mean()

Out[11]: 5.111111111111112

In [12]: # What about the standard deviation (a measure of how dispersed data is)?
         srs.std()

Out[12]: 2.5712081034235856

In [13]: srs.fillna(xbar).std()

Out[13]: 2.2997584414213788
```

The standard deviation went down; this aspect was not preserved. So, we may want to use a different approach to filling in missing information. Perhaps, a way to try this is by randomly generating data with the same mean and standard deviation as the original data. Here, we see a technique that resembles the statistical technique of bootstrapping, where you resample from an existing dataset to emulate its properties in simulated datasets. We begin by generating a brand new dataset, a series that randomly picks numbers from the original series, and also as the index of the missing data, shown as follows:

```
In [14]:  s = srs.std()
          # Generate a NumPy ndarray filled with randomly generated data, of the same length as the missing data
          rep = Series(np.random.choice(srs[srs.notnull()], size=2), index=[5, 7])
          print(rep)

          5    8.0
          7    3.0
          dtype: float64
```

This series is then used for filling in the missing data of the original series:

```
In [15]:  srs.fillna(rep)

Out[15]:  0     2.0
          1     3.0
          2     3.0
          3     9.0
          4     8.0
          5     8.0
          6     8.0
          7     3.0
          8     4.0
          9     4.0
          10    5.0
          dtype: float64
```

The entries 5 and 7 correspond to the series used for filling in the missing data. Now let's compute the means, as follows:

```
In [16]:  srs.fillna(rep).mean()

Out[16]:  5.181818181818182

In [17]:  srs.fillna(rep).std()

Out[17]:  2.56195947736032
```

Neither the mean nor the standard deviation are the same, but the difference between these and the original means and standard deviation is not quite as egregious as before, at least for the standard deviation. Now, obviously with random numbers, this cannot be guaranteed except for large sample sizes.

Let's look at filling in missing information in a DataFrame. For example, here is the DataFrame used previously, where we fill in missing data with 0:

```
In [18]: df.fillna(0)
```

Out[18]:

	AAA	BBB	CCC
0	-0.955540	0.000000	0.740858
1	-0.630479	0.003919	0.000000
2	1.161989	0.389397	0.290482
3	0.000000	0.700840	0.581674
4	0.000000	0.682088	1.438320
5	-2.636118	-1.049945	0.384816
6	1.972780	-0.214350	0.000000

Now, of course you may think there is something problematic with the number 0, so let's look at perhaps filling in missing data with the column means. The command for doing so may resemble the following:

```
In [19]: df.mean()
```

```
Out[19]: AAA    -0.379065
         BBB     0.106958
         CCC     0.467956
         dtype: float64
```

```
In [20]: df.fillna(df.mean())
```

Out[20]:

	AAA	BBB	CCC
0	-0.728469	0.451534	-1.376983
1	-1.130157	1.172551	0.631510
2	0.143993	0.093796	0.467956
3	-0.379065	0.324855	0.467956
4	-1.422367	-0.149822	0.467956
5	-0.379065	0.120375	1.284549
6	1.241677	-1.264587	1.332748

But notice something; the standard deviations have all gone down from what they used to be when we used this approach for filling in missing data!

```
In [21]:  df.std()

Out[21]:  AAA    1.821077
          BBB    0.665239
          CCC    0.454703
          dtype: float64

In [22]:  df.fillna(df.mean()).std()      # ALL standard deviations go down

Out[22]:  AAA    1.486903
          BBB    0.607277
          CCC    0.371263
          dtype: float64
```

We will try the bootstrapping trick that we attempted before. We will fill in missing information with a dictionary, or a `dict`. We will create a `dict` that contains a series for every column with missing information in the DataFrame, and these series will be similar to the series that we generated earlier:

```
In [23]:  col='AAA'
          df[col][df[col].notnull()]

Out[23]:  0    -0.955540
          1    -0.630479
          2     1.161989
          5    -2.636118
          6     1.972780
          Name: AAA, dtype: float64

In [ ]:   # We will fill missing data via a dict
          rep_df = {col: Series(np.random.choice(df[col][df[col].notnull()]),      # Create a Series of random values from col...
                                size=df.isnull()[col].value_counts()[True]),       # ... as many as there are missing values
                                                                                    # in col...
                          index=df[col][df[col].isnull()].index)     # ... and having an index corresponding to the missing values
                                                                      # in the column col of df ...
                    for col in df}    # ... for each column in df
          rep_df
```

Then we fill in the missing information with the data contained in this dictionary:

```
In [25]:  df.fillna(rep_df)
```

	AAA	BBB	CCC
0	-0.955540	-1.049945	0.740858
1	-0.630479	0.003919	0.290482
2	1.161989	0.389397	0.290482
3	1.161989	0.700840	0.581674
4	-2.636118	0.682088	1.438320
5	-2.636118	-1.049945	0.384816
6	1.972780	-0.214350	1.438320

Notice the relationship between the means and the standard deviations:

```
In [26]:  df.fillna(rep_df).mean()

Out[26]:  AAA    -0.365928
          BBB    -0.076857
          CCC     0.737850
          dtype: float64

In [27]:  df.fillna(rep_df).std()

Out[27]:  AAA     1.864750
          BBB     0.743576
          CCC     0.505079
          dtype: float64
```

Summary

In this chapter, we covered arithmetic operations with pandas DataFrames, vectorization, and DataFrame function applications. We also learned how to handle missing data in a pandas DataFrame by deleting or filling in missing information. In the next chapter, we will look at sorting, ranking, and common tasks in data analysis projects.

6
Managing, Indexing, and Plotting

Let's now take a brief look at sorting data using pandas methods. In this chapter, we will be looking at sorting and ranking. Sorting is putting data into various orders, while ranking is finding out which order data would be in if it were sorted. We'll see how to achieve this in pandas. We'll also cover hierarchical indexing and plotting with pandas.

Index sorting

When talking about sorting, we need to think about what exactly we are sorting. There are rows, columns, their indices, and the data they contain. Let's first look at index sorting. We can use the `sort_index` method to rearrange the rows of a DataFrame so that the row indices are in order. We can also sort the columns by setting the access parameter of `sort_index` to 1. By default, sorting is done in ascending order; later rows have larger values than earlier rows, but we can change this behavior by setting the ascending value of the `sort_index` value to false. This sorts in descending order. By default, this is not done in place; you need to set the in place argument of `sort_index` to true for that.

While I have emphasized sorting for DataFrames, sorting a series is effectively the same. Let's see an example. After loading in NumPy and pandas, we create a DataFrame with values to sort, shown in the following screenshot:

```
In [1]:  import numpy as np
         import pandas as pd
         from pandas import Series, DataFrame

In [2]:  df = DataFrame(np.round(np.random.randn(7, 3) * 10),
                        columns=["AAA", "BBB", "CCC"],
                        index=list("defcabg"))
         df
```

Out[2]:

	AAA	BBB	CCC
d	-20.0	12.0	0.0
e	25.0	-5.0	-7.0
f	-1.0	-4.0	-4.0
c	-16.0	12.0	1.0
a	0.0	-3.0	1.0
b	17.0	5.0	10.0
g	4.0	12.0	5.0

Let's sort the index; notice that this is not done in place:

```
In [3]:  df.sort_index()
```

Out[3]:

	AAA	BBB	CCC
a	-19.0	-1.0	-9.0
b	23.0	-4.0	13.0
c	0.0	-5.0	25.0
d	-3.0	3.0	-1.0
e	-5.0	11.0	7.0
f	-13.0	-10.0	-8.0
g	5.0	-17.0	7.0

Let's sort the columns this time, and we will do them in reverse order by setting `ascending=False`; so the first column is now `CCC` and the last is `AAA`, shown as follows:

```
In [4]:  df.sort_index(axis=1, ascending=False)     # Sorting columns by
                                                     # index, opposite
                                                     # order
```

Out[4]:

	CCC	BBB	AAA
d	-1.0	3.0	-3.0
e	7.0	11.0	-5.0
f	-8.0	-10.0	-13.0
c	25.0	-5.0	0.0
a	-9.0	-1.0	-19.0
b	13.0	-4.0	23.0
g	7.0	-17.0	5.0

Sorting by values

If we wish to sort the rows of a DataFrame or the elements of a series, we need to use the `sort_values` method. For a series, you'd call `sort_values` and call it a day. For a DataFrame though, you would need to set the `by` parameter; you can set `by` to a string, indicating the column you want to sort by, or to a list of strings, indicating column names. Sorting will first proceed according to the first column in this list; then, when ties appear, sorting will be according to the next column, and so on.

So, let's demonstrate some of these sorting techniques. We sort the values of the DataFrame according to the column `AAA`, shown in the following screenshot:

```
In [5]:  df.sort_values(by='AAA')      # According to contents of AAA
```

Out[5]:

	AAA	BBB	CCC
a	-19.0	-1.0	-9.0
f	-13.0	-10.0	-8.0
e	-5.0	11.0	7.0
d	-3.0	3.0	-1.0
c	0.0	-5.0	25.0
g	5.0	-17.0	7.0
b	23.0	-4.0	13.0

Notice that all the entries in AAA are now in order, though not much can be said for the other columns. But we can sort according to BBB and break ties according to CCC with the following command. Here is the result:

```
In [6]:  df.sort_values(by=['BBB', 'CCC'])    # Arrange first by BBB,
                                               # breaking ties with CCC
```

Out[6]:

	AAA	BBB	CCC
g	5.0	-17.0	7.0
f	-13.0	-10.0	-8.0
c	0.0	-5.0	25.0
b	23.0	-4.0	13.0
a	-19.0	-1.0	-9.0
d	-3.0	3.0	-1.0
e	-5.0	11.0	7.0

Ranking tells us how the elements would look if they were put in order. We can use the rank method to find the ranking of elements in a series or DataFrame. By default, ranking is done in ascending order; set the ascending argument to false to change this. Ranking is straightforward until ties occur. In such an event, you will need a way to determine the rank. There are four methods for handling ties: average, min, max, and first. Average gives the average rank, min gives the lowest rank possible, max gives the highest possible, and first uses the order in the series to break ties so that they never occur. When called on a DataFrame, each column is ranked individually, and the result will be a DataFrame containing ranks. So now, let's see this ranking in action. We ask for the rank of the entries in df, and this is in fact the result:

```
In [7]:  df.rank()
```

Out[7]:

	AAA	BBB	CCC
d	4.0	6.0	3.0
e	3.0	7.0	4.5
f	2.0	2.0	2.0
c	5.0	3.0	7.0
a	1.0	5.0	1.0
b	7.0	4.0	6.0
g	6.0	1.0	4.5

Notice that we see the rank for each entry of this DataFrame. Now, notice that there were some ties here, in particular for the entry e and the entry g for column CCC. We got the tie broken using average, which is the default, but if we wanted to, we've could set this to max, shown as follows:

In [8]: `df.rank(method="max")`

Out[8]:

	AAA	BBB	CCC
d	4.0	6.0	3.0
e	3.0	7.0	5.0
f	2.0	2.0	2.0
c	5.0	3.0	7.0
a	1.0	5.0	1.0
b	7.0	4.0	6.0
g	6.0	1.0	5.0

As a result, both of these get the fifth place. Up next, we talk about hierarchical indexing.

Hierarchical indexing

We have come a long way, but we're not quite done yet. We need to talk about hierarchical indexing. In this section, we look at hierarchical indices, why they are useful, how they are created, and how they can be used.

So, what are hierarchical indices? They bring additional structure to an index and exist in pandas as MultiIndex class objects, but they are still an index that can be assigned to a series or DataFrame. With a hierarchical index, we think of rows in a DataFrame, or elements in a series, as uniquely identified by combinations of two or more indices. These indices have a hierarchy, and selecting an index at one level will select all elements with that level of the index. We can go on a more theoretical path and claim that when we have a MultiIndex, the dimensionality of the table increases. It behaves, not as a square on which data exists, but as a cube, or at least it could.

A hierarchical index is used when we want additional structure on the index without treating that structure as a new column. One way to create a `MultiIndex` is to use the initialization method of the `MultiIndex` object in pandas. We can also create a `MultiIndex` implicitly when creating a pandas series or DataFrame, by passing a list of lists to the `index` argument, each of them having the same length as the series. Either method is acceptable, but we will have an `index` object we assign to the series or DataFrame we're creating in the first case; while in the second, the series and `MultiIndex` are created simultaneously.

Let's create some hierarchical indices. After importing pandas and NumPy, we create a `MultiIndex` directly using the `MultiIndex` object. Now, this notation may be somewhat difficult to read, so let's create this index and explain what just happened:

```
In [1]: import pandas as pd
        from pandas import Series, DataFrame
        import numpy as np

In [2]: # Directly with MultiIndex
        midx = pd.MultiIndex([['a', 'b'], ['alpha', 'beta'], [1, 2]],
                             [[0, 0, 0, 0, 1, 1, 1, 1],
                              [0, 0, 1, 1, 0, 0, 1, 1],
                              [0, 1, 0, 1, 0, 1, 0, 1]])
        Series(np.arange(8), index=midx)

Out[2]: a  alpha  1    0
                  2    1
           beta   1    2
                  2    3
        b  alpha  1    4
                  2    5
           beta   1    6
                  2    7
        dtype: int32
```

Here, we assign the levels of the index, that is, possible values the `MultiIndex` can take. So, we have for the first level, a and b; for the second level, `alpha` and `beta`; and for the third level, 1 and 2. Then we assign, for each row of this `MultiIndex`, which of these levels are taken. So, each of the zeros for this first list indicates the value a, and each of the ones for this list indicates the value b. Then we have zeros for `alpha` and ones for `beta` in the second list. In the third list, we have zeros for 1 and ones for 2. And thus, you end up with this object after assigning `midx` to the index of series.

Another way to create a `MultiIndex` is directly when we are creating the series we're interested in. Here, the `index` argument has been passed multiple lists, each of those lists being a part of a `MulitIndex`.

The first line will be for the first level of the `MulitIndex`, the second line for the second level, and the third line for the third level. It's very similar to what we did in the earlier case, but instead of having the levels explicitly defined and then defining which of the levels are for each value of the series, we simply put in the values that we are interested in:

```
In [3]: # In the Series creation
        srs = Series(np.arange(8),
                        index=[['a', 'a', 'a', 'a', 'b', 'b', 'b', 'b'],
                        ['alpha', 'alpha', 'beta', 'beta',
                         'alpha', 'alpha', 'beta', 'beta'],
                        [1, 2, 1, 2, 1, 2, 1, 2]])

        srs

Out[3]: a   alpha   1     0
                    2     1
            beta    1     2
                    2     3
        b   alpha   1     4
                    2     5
            beta    1     6
                    2     7
        dtype: int32
```

Notice that these produce identical results.

Slicing a series with a hierarchical index

When it comes to slicing, series of the hierarchical index resemble NumPy multidimensional arrays. For example, if using the square bracket accessor, we simply separate levels of the hierarchical index with commas, and slice each level, imagining that they were separate indices for separate dimensions of some high-dimensional object. This holds for the `loc` method as well as for series, but not for DataFrames; we'll see what to do there later. All the usual tricks when slicing indices still work when using `loc`, but it's easier to get multiple results for a slicing operation.

So, let's see slicing a series of the `MultiIndex` in action. The first thing we're going to do is slice the first level, selecting only those elements where the first level is b; this is the result:

```
In [4]:  srs.loc['b']

Out[4]:  alpha  1    4
                2    5
         beta   1    6
                2    7
         dtype: int32
```

Then we narrow it down further to b and alpha; the following is the result. It's going to be the alpha segment (in the preceding screenshot) of the series:

```
In [5]:  srs.loc['b', 'alpha']      # The following won't work for DataFrames

Out[5]:  1    4
         2    5
         dtype: int32
```

Then we select it even further, so we have to go three levels if we want to select one particular element of this series, as follows:

```
In [6]:  srs.loc['b', 'alpha', 1]

Out[6]:  4
```

If we wish to select every element of the series, such that the first level is a and the last level is 1, we will need to put a colon in the middle to indicate that we don't care whether we have alpha or beta, and this is the result:

```
In [7]:  srs.loc['a', :, 1]

Out[7]:  a  alpha  1    0
            beta   1    2
         dtype: int32
```

When a hierarchical index is present for a DataFrame, we can still use the `loc` method for indexing, but doing so is trickier than for series. After all, we can't separate levels of the index by commas because we have a second dimension, columns. So we use tuples to provide instructions for slicing one of the dimensions of the DataFrame, providing the objects that instruct how to slice. Each element of the tuple could be a number, a string, or a list of desired elements.

We cannot really use the colon notation when using tuples; we will need to rely on slicers. We see here how to replicate some of the slicing notation commonly used with slicers. We can pass these slicers on to the elements of the tuple used for slicing so that we can do the slicing operations we like. If we want to select all columns, we will still need to provide a colon in the columns' position in `loc`. Naturally, we can replace the slicers with a more specific means for slicing, such as a list or a single element. Now, I never talked about what would happen if columns had a hierarchical index. That's because the lessons are essentially the same—because columns are just an index on a different axis.

So now let's look at managing a hierarchical index attached to a DataFrame. The first thing we do is create a DataFrame with a hierarchical index. Then we select all rows where the first level of this index is b. We get the following result, which is not too shocking:

In [8]:
```
df = DataFrame(np.random.randn(8, 3), index=midx,
               columns=['AAA', 'BBB', 'CCC'])
df.loc['b']
```

Out[8]:

		AAA	BBB	CCC
alpha	1	1.340283	1.481745	-0.407162
	2	-0.123670	0.568047	0.601709
beta	1	1.025617	-0.697987	0.444483
	2	-1.256752	0.001763	0.121052

And then we repeat by narrowing down by `b` and `alpha`, but notice that we now have to use a tuple in order to ensure that alpha is not being interpreted as a column that we're interested in, shown as follows:

```
In [9]: df.loc[('b', 'alpha')]    # Must use a tuple here
Out[9]:
```

	AAA	BBB	CCC
1	1.340283	1.481745	-0.407162
2	-0.123670	0.568047	0.601709

Then we narrow down even further, as follows:

```
In [10]:  df.loc[('b', 'alpha', 1)]

Out[10]:  AAA     1.340283
          BBB     1.481745
          CCC    -0.407162
          Name: (b, alpha, 1), dtype: float64
```

Now, let's try to replicate some of the things that we did before, but recall that we can no longer use the colon notation here; we have to use slicers. So the slicing call that we are going to use here is identical to the slicing call that we used in `srs.loc['b', 'alpha', 1]`. I say `slice(None)`, which basically means select everything in the second level:

```
In [11]: df.loc[('b', slice(None), 1), :]    # Don't treat : as optional
Out[11]:
```

			AAA	BBB	CCC
	alpha	1	1.340283	1.481745	-0.407162
b					
	beta	1	1.025617	-0.697987	0.444483

And we do have to put a colon in the columns position if we intend to select all columns; otherwise an error will be thrown. Here, we're going to do what is effectively the equivalent of using `:'b'`, so we are selecting from the very beginning up to `b`. This is the result:

```
In [12]:  df.loc[(slice(None, 'b'), slice(None), 1), ['AAA', 'BBB']]   # : 'b'
```

Out[12]:

			AAA	BBB
a	alpha	1	0.371582	0.061726
	beta	1	0.076597	-1.190527
b	alpha	1	1.340283	1.481745
	beta	1	1.025617	-0.697987

Finally, we select everything in the first level and everything in the second level, but we're going to be specific only in the third level, shown as follows:

```
In [13]:  df.loc[(slice(None), slice(None), 1), 'CCC']

Out[13]: a  alpha  1     1.821459
            beta   1     1.121959
         b  alpha  1    -0.407162
            beta   1     0.444483
Name: CCC, dtype: float64
```

And notice that we have been passing indexing calls to the columns as well, because this is an entirely separate call. We now move on to using plotting methods provided by pandas.

Plotting with pandas

In this section, we will be discussing the plotting methods provided by pandas series and DataFrames. You will see how to easily and quickly create a number of useful plots. pandas has not yet come up with plotting functionality that's entirely its own. Rather, plots created from pandas objects using pandas methods are just wrappers for more complex calls made to a plotting library called **Matplotlib**. This is a well-known library in the scientific Python community, one of the first plotting systems, and perhaps the most commonly used one, though other plotting systems are looking to supplant it.

It was initially inspired by the plotting system provided with MATLAB, though now it is its own beast, but not necessarily the easiest to use. Matplotlib has a lot of functionality, and we will only scratch the surface of plotting with it in this course. This section is the extent to which we discuss visualization with Python beyond particular instances, even though visualization is a key part of data analysis, from initial exploration to presenting results. I recommend looking for other resources to learn more about visualization. For example, Packt has video courses devoted exclusively to this topic.

Anyway, if we want to be able to plot using pandas methods, Matplotlib must be installed and available for use. If you're using a Jupyter Notebook or the Jupyter QtConsole, or some other IPython-based environment, I would recommend running the `pylab` magic.

Plotting methods

The key pandas objects, series, and DataFrames come supplied with a plotting method, simply known as plot. It can easily create plots such as line plots, scatter plots, bar charts, or what are known as kernel density estimation plots (used to get a sense of the shape of the data), and so on. There are many plots that can be created. We can control which plot we want by setting the kind parameter in `plot`, to a string, indicating which plot we want. Often this produces some plot with usually well-chosen default parameters. We can have more control over the final output by specifying other parameters in the plot method, which are then passed on to Matplotlib. Thus we can control issues such as labeling, the style of the plot, *x* limits, *y* limits, opacity, and other details.

Other methods exist for creating different plots; for example, series have a method called hist for creating histograms.

In this Notebook, I'm going to demonstrate what some plots look like. The first thing I'll be doing is loading in `pandas`, and I will be using the `pylab` magic, the Matplotlib magic with the parameter inline, so that we can see plots the moment they are created:

```
In [1]:  import pandas as pd
         from pandas import Series, DataFrame
         # Loads NumPy and matplotlib for interactive use
         %pylab
         # Shows matplotlib objects inline
         %matplotlib inline

         Using matplotlib backend: Qt4Agg
         Populating the interactive namespace from numpy and matplotlib
```

Now, we create a DataFrame that contains three random walks, which is a process that's studied and used in probability theory. A random walk can be generated by creating standard normal random variables and then summing them up cumulatively, as shown here:

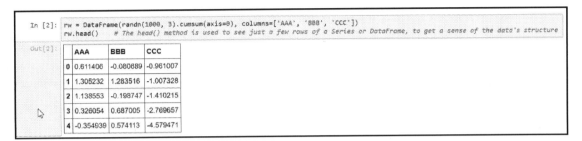

```
In [2]: rw = DataFrame(randn(1000, 3).cumsum(axis=0), columns=['AAA', 'BBB', 'CCC'])
        rw.head()    # The head() method is used to see just a few rows of a Series or DataFrame, to get a sense of the data's structure
```

Out[2]:

	AAA	BBB	CCC
0	0.611406	-0.080689	-0.961007
1	1.305232	1.283516	-1.007328
2	1.138553	-0.198747	-1.410215
3	0.326054	0.687005	-2.769657
4	-0.354939	0.574113	-4.579471

We use the head method to see only the first five rows. This is a good way to get a sense of the structure of the dataset. So, what do these plots look like? Well, let's create a line plot that visualizes them, illustrated as follows:

```
In [3]: rw.shape

Out[3]: (1000, 3)
```

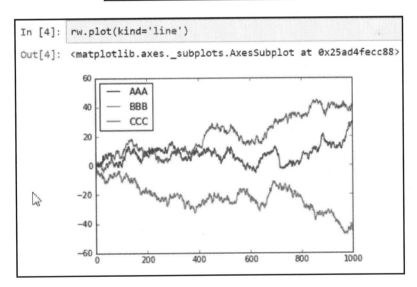

```
In [4]: rw.plot(kind='line')

Out[4]: <matplotlib.axes._subplots.AxesSubplot at 0x25ad4fecc88>
```

These are just random movements, up and down. Notice that the plot method automatically generated a key and a legend and assigned colors to the different lines, which correspond to columns of the DataFrame from which we're plotting. Let's see what this plot looks like for a series, shown as follows:

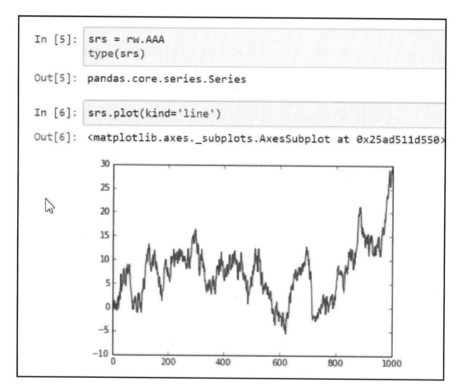

It's a little less advanced but as you can see, we can still create these plots using series.

Let's specify a parameter, ylim, so that the scale of the plot from the series is the same as the scale of the plot for the DataFrame, shown as follows:

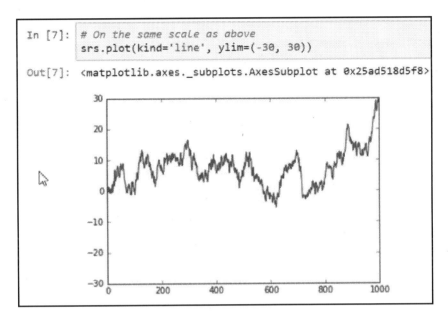

```
In [7]:  # On the same scale as above
         srs.plot(kind='line', ylim=(-30, 30))

Out[7]:  <matplotlib.axes._subplots.AxesSubplot at 0x25ad518d5f8>
```

Now let's look at some different plots. In the next screenshot, let's look at the histogram of the values that are in this series:

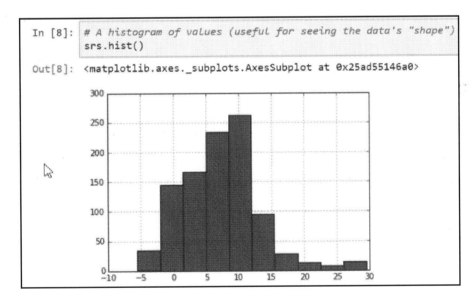

```
In [8]:  # A histogram of values (useful for seeing the data's "shape")
         srs.hist()

Out[8]:  <matplotlib.axes._subplots.AxesSubplot at 0x25ad55146a0>
```

A histogram is a useful way to determine the shape of a dataset. Here, we see a roughly symmetrical, almost bell curve shape.

We can also create a histogram using the `plot` method, as follows:

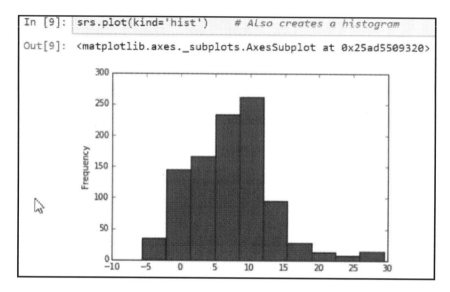

```
In [9]: srs.plot(kind='hist')    # Also creates a histogram

Out[9]: <matplotlib.axes._subplots.AxesSubplot at 0x25ad5509320>
```

A kernel density estimator is effectively a smooth histogram. With a histogram, you create bins and count how many observations in your dataset fell into those bins. The kernel density estimator uses a different way to create the plot, but what you end up with is a smooth curve, shown as follows:

```
In [*]: # Compare this to a "smoothed" histogram, a kernel density estimation plot
        srs.plot(kind='kde')
```

Let's look at some other plots. For example, we create box plots for the DataFrame:

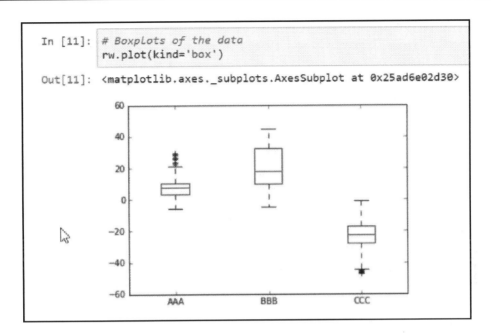

```
In [11]:   # Boxplots of the data
           rw.plot(kind='box')
```

```
Out[11]:   <matplotlib.axes._subplots.AxesSubplot at 0x25ad6e02d30>
```

We can also create scatter plots, and when creating a scatter plot, we will need to specify which column corresponds to x values and which column corresponds to y values:

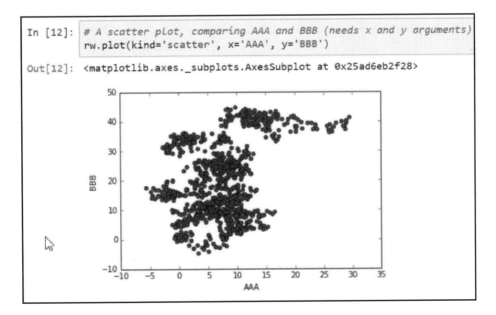

```
In [12]:   # A scatter plot, comparing AAA and BBB (needs x and y arguments)
           rw.plot(kind='scatter', x='AAA', y='BBB')
```

```
Out[12]:   <matplotlib.axes._subplots.AxesSubplot at 0x25ad6eb2f28>
```

There are a lot of data points here. Another approach would be to use what's called a hex-bin plot, which you can think of as a 2D histogram; it counts the observations that have fallen into certain hexagonal bins on the real plane, shown as follows:

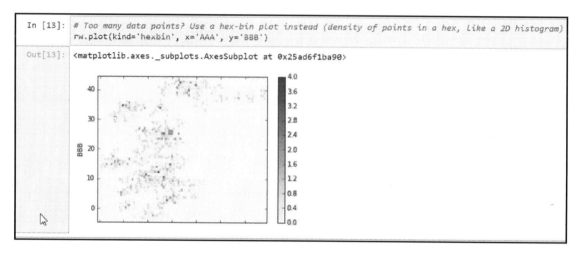

Now, this hex plot doesn't seem to be very useful, so let's set the grid size to 25:

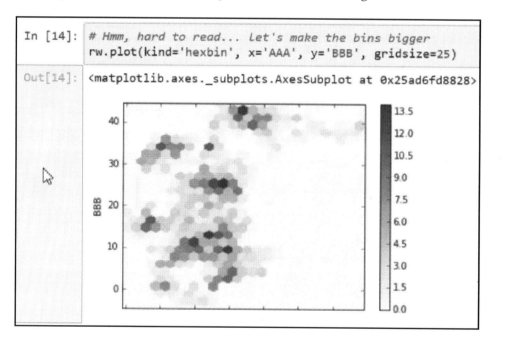

Now we have a much more interesting plot, and we can see where the data tends to cluster. Let's compute the standard deviation of each column in the plot, as follows:

```
In [15]:  # Comparing standard deviations of each column with a bar plot
          rw.std()

Out[15]:  AAA        5.804459
          BBB       12.936209
          CCC        9.516350
          dtype: float64
```

And now, let's create a bar plot to visualize these standard deviations, as follows:

```
In [16]:  rw.std().plot(kind='bar')

Out[16]:  <matplotlib.axes._subplots.AxesSubplot at 0x25ad70abc88>
```

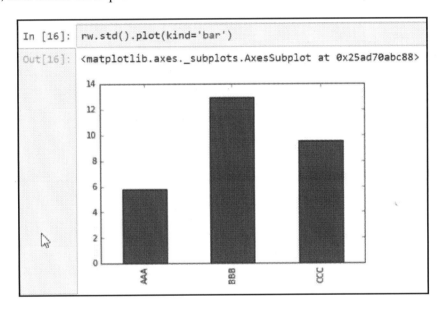

Now, let's look at a slightly more advanced tool called a **scatter plot matrix**, which can be useful for visualizing multiple relationships in a dataset, as follows:

```
In [*]:   # A scatterplot matrix, for visualizing multiple relationships
          pd.tools.plotting.scatter_matrix(rw)
```

```
Out[17]:  array([[<matplotlib.axes._subplots.AxesSubplot object at 0x0000025AD70EBF60>,
                  <matplotlib.axes._subplots.AxesSubplot object at 0x0000025AD7171CF8>,
                  <matplotlib.axes._subplots.AxesSubplot object at 0x0000025AD71BDE48>],
                 [<matplotlib.axes._subplots.AxesSubplot object at 0x0000025AD71F8F98>,
                  <matplotlib.axes._subplots.AxesSubplot object at 0x0000025AD7245BA8>,
                  <matplotlib.axes._subplots.AxesSubplot object at 0x0000025AD7283278>],
                 [<matplotlib.axes._subplots.AxesSubplot object at 0x0000025AD72C8F98>,
                  <matplotlib.axes._subplots.AxesSubplot object at 0x0000025AD72D8940>,
                  <matplotlib.axes._subplots.AxesSubplot object at 0x0000025AD7356B70>]], dtype=object)
```

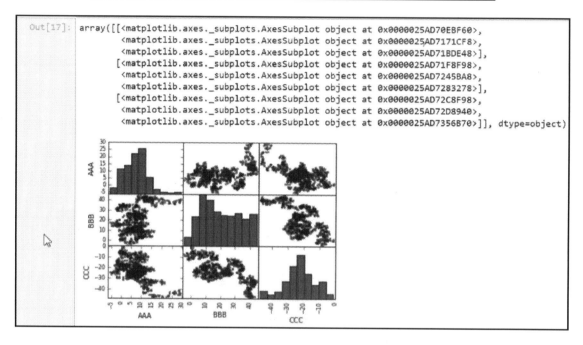

There are many more plots that you can create; I seriously invite you to explore plotting methods, not only those for pandas (for which I have provided a link to the documentation with numerous examples) but also those for Matplotlib.

Summary

In this chapter, we started with index sorting and saw how sorting can be done by values. We covered hierarchical clustering and slicing a series with a hierarchical index. In the end, we saw various plotting methods and demonstrated them.

We've come a long way. We've set up a Python data analysis environment and gotten familiar with basic tools. All the best!

Other Books You May Enjoy

If you enjoyed this book, you may be interested in these other books by Packt:

Pandas Cookbook
Theodore Petrou

ISBN: 978-1-78439-387-8

- Master the fundamentals of pandas to quickly begin exploring any dataset
- Isolate any subset of data by properly selecting and querying the data
- Split data into independent groups before applying aggregations and transformations to each group
- Restructure data into tidy form to make data analysis and visualization easier
- Prepare real-world messy datasets for machine learning
- Combine and merge data from different sources through pandas SQL-like operations
- Utilize pandas unparalleled time series functionality
- Create beautiful and insightful visualizations through pandas direct hooks to matplotlib and seaborn

Hands-On Data Science with Anaconda
Dr. Yuxing Yan, James Yan

ISBN: 978-1-78883-119-2

- Perform cleaning, sorting, classification, clustering, regression, and dataset modeling using Anaconda
- Use the package manager conda and discover, install, and use functionally efficient and scalable packages
- Get comfortable with heterogeneous data exploration using multiple languages within a project
- Perform distributed computing and use Anaconda Accelerate to optimize computational powers
- Discover and share packages, notebooks, and environments, and use shared project drives on Anaconda Cloud
- Tackle advanced data prediction problems

Leave a review - let other readers know what you think

Please share your thoughts on this book with others by leaving a review on the site that you bought it from. If you purchased the book from Amazon, please leave us an honest review on this book's Amazon page. This is vital so that other potential readers can see and use your unbiased opinion to make purchasing decisions, we can understand what our customers think about our products, and our authors can see your feedback on the title that they have worked with Packt to create. It will only take a few minutes of your time, but is valuable to other potential customers, our authors, and Packt. Thank you!

Index